Teaching Riding

TEACHING RIDING

JOSEPHINE KNOWLES F.B.H.S.

J. A. ALLEN
London

British Library Cataloguing-in-Publication Data.
A catalogue record for this book is available from the British Library.

ISBN 0–85131–744–8

© J. A. Allen & Co. Ltd., 1999

No part of this book may be reproduced, stored in a retrieval system, or transmitted, in any form or by any means, electronic, mechanical, photocopying, recording or otherwise, without the prior permission of the publisher. All rights reserved.

Published in Great Britain in 1999 by
J. A. Allen & Company Limited
1 Lower Grosvenor Place
London SW1W 0EL

Printed in Great Britain by Hillman Printers Ltd., Frome.

Contents

Introduction   vii

1 Teaching   1
Your personality—Your voice—Teaching individual characters—Teaching at Pony Club/riding club rallies or camps—Teaching anywhere

2 Potential dangers   7
Inspecting tack for safety—Teaching new pupils—Teaching jumping—Common causes of falls—Falls out on a hack—Dealing with falls—Sensible safety precautions—Teaching dismounted—Dangers on foot—Accident book

3 The rider's position in the saddle   19
The pelvis that a rider sits on—Saddles and position

4 The conformation of the rider   28
Short back—Long back—Long legs, lean flat thighs—Short legs, round thighs—Short arms—Long arms—Overweight—Round shoulders—Collapsed back—Head and neck poking forward Hollow back—Collapsed hip, sitting crooked—Toes out—Toes in when standing—One leg longer than the other—Weak ankles

5 Bits and reins   44
Lessons on pupils' own horses—Length of reins—Grass reins

6 Whips and hands   54
The correct position of a whip—Hands—Transitions

7 Riding faults   71
Hands crossing over neck—Leg position—Use of spurs—Legs—Teaching beginners to trot—Lungeing the rider—Rising trot

8 Canter   94

9 Teaching control   103
Steadying and stopping—On the bit—Turn on the forehand—Turn on the haunches—Rein back

10 Saddlery   119
Martingales—Nosebands—Double bridle

11 Lessons using barrels or cones   128
Riding in traffic—Shying—Kicking—Out on a hack

12 Trotting poles   139
Fan shape

13 Jumping   144
Holding the mane—Holding a neckstrap—Teaching beginners to jump—Guiding and controlling—A course of jumps for novice riders—Horses that refuse—Young horses—Teaching adults

14 Teaching can be fun   165
Teaching boys—Pony Club camp/rallies: the youngest ride—Teach about safety and danger—Teaching but also amusing and interesting your ride—Teaching but also amusing and interesting your ride when jumping—Showing

Conclusion   184

Index   185

Introduction

I have written this book because I want all instructors, of whatever standard, to know how important it is for them to be able to think and feel what is happening mentally and physically to the horses that they ride. I want them to understand the meaning of sitting in balance with their horses and how the horses are affected enormously and are sensitive to the tiniest change of their weight.

Only if *they* can think, feel and understand the importance of this themselves can they explain and convey it to their pupils.

The basic lessons on position in this book are not only for beginners and novice pupils. It is a sad but true fact that many people who have ridden for years cannot think, feel and understand the meaning of sitting in balance with their horse.

There is often resentment when an instructor, who has been asked to help a client to school their horse, says that they cannot improve the horse until the pupil's basic position is correct and therefore that must be worked on first.

It has been known for clients to say, "I am not paying you to teach me, I am paying you to teach my horse."!

The rider must sit correctly in the saddle in balance with the horse and understand the feel of being out of balance. They must also understand the mental and physical effect of sudden changes of their weight, however slight, before they can progress to being taught how to school their horse successfully.

Only when a rider can sit in balance with the horse and understand the feel of this can they learn to coordinate their aids sufficiently to perform simple but smooth transitions or changes of direction. The foundation of sitting in balance must be sound before there can be successful progress to more advanced work on the flat or to jumping.

I hope that the methods, thoughts, suggestions and explanations in this book will help all people who teach, whether for a living, to pass exams or to help friends or relatives to understand more about their own riding and therefore have a clearer idea of how to teach and help others.

Josephine Knowles
1999

1   Teaching

Your personality

It is very easy to think that having completed a course and passed an exam you know a lot and really can teach riding. The longer you live the more you realise how little you know so the more you learn. If you have an open mind, watch and observe horses and riders carefully and thoughtfully and really work out how and why various things happen each day, your teaching will improve much more quickly.

You must really enjoy teaching. You must like horses but you must also like and be interested in people, even the most trying ones! You must be something of a psychologist and try to work out the characters of your pupils, help the nervous to gain confidence, make the aggressive rider more gentle and feeling, make the "wimp" more positive, quieten the bossy and bring out the timid. You must notice if someone is "riding out of character", they may be feeling ill or very tired or they may have a problem at home. Be sympathetic – don't "get at" them.

Plan your lessons carefully, make them interesting and progressive and go through them in your mind afterwards. What went well and really worked an improvement? What didn't work or even made something worse? Did they enjoy it? Were there some light hearted moments?

Don't be so rigid that you keep to your original plan even if something unexpected and interesting happens in the lesson. An impromptu occurrence can often produce a really practical interesting lesson. Why did it occur? Ask questions. What are the possible reasons? What can we do? Would that work? The whole class can be involved in thinking it out, then trying out the suggestions. That is good teaching.

I think it is very difficult to give individual help to a class lesson of more than eight people. People learn from watching but the watching must not last too long and the watchers must know they are going to be questioned on what they have seen or most of them won't watch!

Your voice

The voice is all important. It can bore people to sleep and switch them off, it can frighten them and make them stiffen. Your voice can make your pupils think only of you and your aggressive shouts instead of how their horse feels under them. It can wake them up and make them alert by changes of tone and pitch or make them feel really good and try even harder by praise. It can be so quiet that some people can't hear and dare not say so. It can be squashing and sarcastic. It can go into such a complicated explanation that no one has any idea what you are talking about although you have gone on for fifteen minutes. Your voice can be an asset or a disaster. Think about it and if possible improve it by recording and then listening to yourself instructing.

Cut your explanations down to a few simple words, sometimes using an uncomplicated comparison not connected with riding which your pupils can visualise and understand easily. Demonstrate more – talk less. Question more. Make them think. If something looks as if it is better ask them, "Can you feel the difference?" Teaching should develop the riders' feel for what is going on underneath them. It should also develop their understanding of how the horse's body works and what the horse thinks and feels when the rider changes their weight and uses rein and leg aids.

Try out the exercises you are going to use and the faults and then corrections that you give to the riders when sitting on a horse yourself. See how they work for you. Do they help or do they make you feel that your body or limbs are now stiffer?

If instructors tried things out on themselves first I am sure they would not use the type of truly disastrous exercise I was asked to perform as a pupil – which I know made me feel very stiff and ride with much less softness and feel. For instance, I have often seen instructors put canes or sticks across the front of pupils' elbows and behind their backs pinning their arms back in a forced fixed position to make them sit up straight. This totally fixes their hands, elbows and shoulders and makes their backs rigid. How can they feel and follow the movement of the horse's head like this? I cannot believe that anyone who tells their ride to do this had tried it out for themselves. Try it yourself and I am quite sure that you will hate the feeling it gives and realise what a disastrous idea it is.

Another exercise I was asked to do as a pupil and always felt was totally wrong was to hold a stick in both hands parallel to the ground while holding both reins. The idea of the exercise was supposed to be, "To see who can keep their hands still."

If you say, "Keep your hands still," pupils are likely to fix their hands and stiffen their wrist, elbow and shoulder joints, so don't do it. Say, "Keep your reins in a straight line." Their attention now goes to their reins and to keep the reins in a straight line they must follow the action of the horse's head and move their hands and so their elbow and shoulder joints. If they keep their hands "still" their reins will go loose, tight, loose, tight. This is especially obvious at walk and canter where the horse uses more head movement than at trot.

When holding a stick in this way, knuckles upwards, the rider's forearm is twisted into an unnatural position and a stiffness can be felt in wrist, elbow and shoulder joints. The suppleness felt in the thumbs on top, fingernails towards each other position is lost. In this flat-handed, knuckles

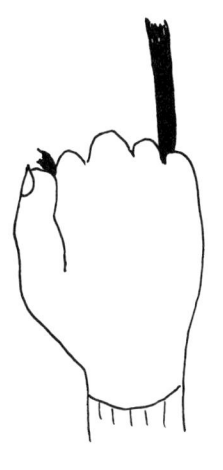

Incorrect position of flat hands with the knuckles on top.

on top, position it is much more difficult to follow the movement of the horse's head and "Keep the reins in a straight line."

Try them out yourself and see what you feel about these exercises even if you have never used them before. They will make you realise how very important it is for the instructor to know the "feel" of the exercises and corrections that they give to their ride and how some can be a disaster.

Teaching is a "sixty seconds to the minute" job. It is very tiring because you must never stop concentrating, thinking, anticipating danger before it happens, having "eyes in the back of your head" and above all giving praise whenever praise is due.

Be positive. Try not to keep saying, "*Don't* do this or that." It is depressing. "Raise (or lift) your inside hand," is much better than "Don't drop your inside hand."

Always say the rider's name first to get their attention before making a correction or praising. When a correction has made a rider look much better ask them to go out alone and show the others: "Look at the difference that has made to Mary. Does it feel better?"

Try not to have favourites nor to ignore those pupils who will never make riders however hard you work. Try not to "get at" bolshie or uncooperative individuals as it will only make them worse!

Teaching individual characters

Sum up the character of each person in your ride. If you have a bolshie individual make them leading file, praise their pony, praise them – be nice to them and they may cooperate. Don't try to *make* a child, or an adult, do something they are frightened of; be prepared to alter your plan or change a fence for a nervous person or a young horse. Treat them as individuals. If a certain exercise would be good for half the ride but make the others worse tell them not to do it and explain why.

If two people have the same fault pair them up and divide the ride so that one half of each pair rides while the other half watches then they can see the fault in the other person and watch the difference after a correction. There is then competition to see who can improve most. Be very quick to praise the slightest improvement and after an individual's correction look for a reason to praise them.

Try to keep the ride relaxed, thinking and feeling. Explain what you are going to do and why. Explain faults and that they do not necessarily originate where they show. Train pupils to notice good and bad points about ponies and riders. Involve them by asking for suggestions to correct faults and then discuss their answers. Even eight-year-olds can be really interested and become critical and observant.

Do give enough praise – even the slightest improvement should receive favourable comment particularly as this often produces even more effort to improve further. Whatever the lesson, try to finish on a good note and if all has gone really well ignore pleas for "Just once more" or "Just a bit higher, wider, faster." It is surprising how often that last "go" can produce an accident or at least a problem which needs time to sort out – and there won't be time to do so.

Teaching at Pony Club/riding club rallies or camps

Whenever you are going to take a ride of people unknown to you on their own horses or ponies make quick notes on the colour of their horse or its unusual markings, the riders' hair or figure, or special tack or boots to help you remember peoples' names. It definitely pays to take the trouble to learn and remember names because there is then a more personal feeling between you and your ride. Giving them numbers is totally impersonal.

A leather punch will be an essential piece of equipment, also several pieces of foam to use as wither pads or to lift the back of saddles.

Teaching anywhere

Remember that there are various ways of saying the same thing:

1. Toes up. Heels down.
2. Lift your hand. Bend your elbow.
3. Keep your reins in a straight line. Have a contact with your horse's mouth.

4. (Usually to be preceded by, "Sit further forward in the saddle.") Bend your knee more. Keep your lower leg further back towards your horse's tail. Think of kneeling.
5. Sit further forward in the saddle. Sit as close to the pommel as you can. Imagine that there is an upturned drawing pin near the back of the saddle. If you sit too far back you will get pricked by it.
6. Let your weight drop into your seat, not onto your stirrup irons. Try not to push against the stirrups. Your lower leg is coming forward because you are stiffening your knee and bracing against your stirrups.
7. (Rising trot.) Sit gently in the saddle as you go down. Just touch the saddle as you go down. Try not to sit down heavily with your lower leg coming forward because you will find it difficult to heave yourself up again to rise. Think of getting up from a chair. It is much easier to do so if your feet are back under you and very difficult if your feet and legs are sticking out in front of you.
8. Sit up tall. Take a deep breath. Get your head closer to the roof/sky.
9. (For collapsed back.) Let the top of your pelvis come forward. Stick your tummy out. Hollow your back. Think of leaning back against a garden bench which holds the middle of your back forward.
10. (For hollow back, tipping forward or sitting on the fork.) Push or tuck your tummy in. Tuck your bottom underneath you more. Get the waistband at the back of your jods closer to the back of the saddle.
11. Put more weight into your inside seat bone. Put your inside heel down more.
12. Bring your outside shoulder forward. Keep your shoulders parallel with the horse's shoulders.

These are just a few examples. I am sure you will think of many more. Changing the words you use is necessary because all riders' minds work differently and you must get the message through to as many as possible.

2 Potential dangers

No one, of course, is able to list all the dangers that can be present when you are instructing a ride. But experience and good practice help in the prevention of danger.

I list below some of those dangers I have met with and ways of dealing with them.

1. A long loop of end of reins hanging down below the level of the rider's foot. It may get caught round their foot and if they fall off their foot can be held in the stirrup by the loop of rein. This has happened and a child was dragged. Check the loop of the reins again after the stirrups have been shortened for jumping.
2. Loose girths causing the saddle to slip round. Check girths before and after the rider mounts. Check during the ride and always before jumping. Be especially careful to watch out for saddles slipping round on fat, circular ponies. Check girths frequently on hacks.

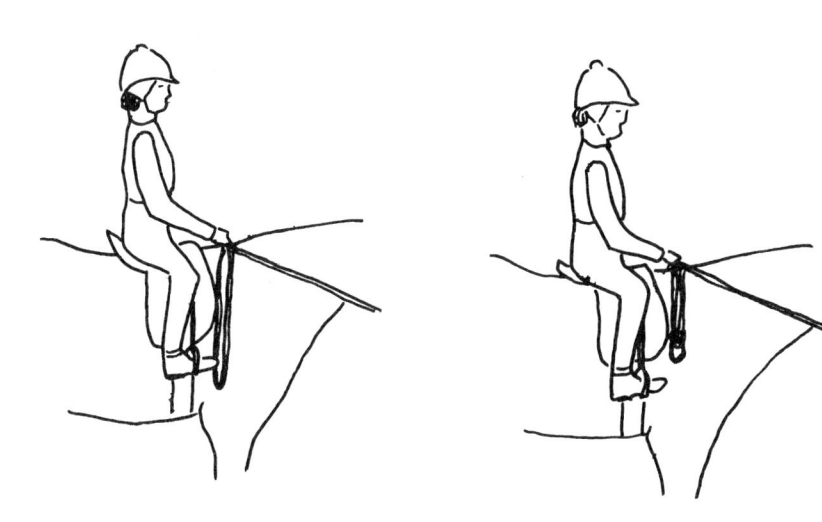

Danger: (far left) *the loop of reins is too long. The loop could get caught round a rider's foot;* (left) *to avoid this, put a knot in the loop. Then check the length of loops again after the stirrups have been shortened for jumping.*

3. Saddles slipping forward up the neck of little fat ponies who have no shoulder. Look out especially when going downhill.
4. Saddles slipping back on "herring gutted" horses which run up narrower behind the girth allowing the girth and saddle to slip back. Watch out for this happening when going uphill and when jumping.
5. Are the stirrup irons big enough for the rider's foot? Feet get stuck in small stirrups.
6. Nickel stirrups are not safe. They can break and the sharp ends could then go into the rider's foot. If the horse falls nickel can bend and trap the rider's foot. Nickel stirrups can bend and gradually weaken and break. Safety stirrup irons can bend and open up.
7. Nickel bits can bend and break and often do so.
8. Foreign rubber bits often have no strengthening chain through the centre and can break.
9. Check the bend in the stirrup leathers where the stirrup hangs; leather can crack here and break. Check the holes in stirrup leathers to see if any have split and lengthened. Worn stirrup leathers should be thrown away. Check the buckles to see that the prong holds safely and is not bent. Check the stitching.
10. Check girths for strength and safety. Check the buckles. Check the stitching.
11. Check saddles for broken trees and check the girth straps to see if they are cracked and worn. See if any holes have lengthened or split. Check the webbings which attach the girth straps to the saddle, one for the front girth strap, another for the two back ones.
12. Find out if any animals in a ride unknown to you are likely to kick. Notice if any mares in your ride are in season and keep all other horses at double distance from them if necessary.
13. Do not allow riders to carry buckets, haynets, rattly boxes or anything flapping when riding a horse until the horse has been tested without a rider on it to see if it is nervous of the object. Warn riders to drop the object immediately if the horse is frightened by it.
14. Do not allow riders to take their coats or jerseys off or put them on when mounted unless someone is holding their horse and it is a quiet and sensible animal.

15. Do not allow riders to do exercises such as "round the world" unless their horse is being held by a capable person.
16. When taking a ride of privately-owned horses or ponies be exceptionally careful if you want your riders to change ponies. Always match pony and rider with thought and care and do not take risks with more lively mounts.
17. Do not allow riders to follow each other over trotting poles. Call them in by name so that if there is a problem the next person will not have started to come.
18. Do not let riders follow on over jumps. It makes some animals excitable and if there is a problem there could be a pile up. (An experienced horse and rider giving a young horse a lead is permissible.)
19. Remove unused jump cups from fences and put them where they cannot be stepped on or fallen on to. They can damage horse and rider.
20. It is safer to always use an upright at each end of a wall jump or anything solid. If the horse tries to run out and jumps the corner awkwardly the rider can fall off onto the corner of the wall and be injured.
21. Milk crates as fillers or supporting a low pole can be a danger to horse and rider.
22. Poles supported by straw bales or barrels should always rest right at the edge of the landing side so that they will fall easily if knocked. (If they are in the centre they could just roll forward without falling and bring a horse down.)
23. Cavalletti can roll and be dangerous. They do not fall cleanly if piled up and could bring a horse down. Using them without thought has caused several accidents.
24. Barrels, if used as a filler, should be strong and sound. They should have poles on the ground on each side of them to stop them rolling. Straw bales are dangerous if piled one on top of another.
25. If the ground is slippery when you are taking a ride outside don't try to canter them round the school. Send them out one at a time to canter in a straight line to a given point away from the ride and walk back. Only do this canter if the ground is fit.
26. Do not allow your pupils to canter towards home after a lesson or

when out on a hack. An excitable horse may speed up and the rest of the ride will follow. When this happens it is likely to cause accidents.
27. Horses have moods, just like people do. Notice any change in a horse's normal behaviour and if necessary change your lesson or hack plan accordingly.
28. Normally quiet animals can behave very differently in a high wind. If you don't stay alert all the time and foresee danger accidents could happen.

Inspecting tack for safety

1. Check holes in stirrup leathers for splits.
2. Check the bend of stirrup leathers, where stirrups hang, for cracks.
3. Check girth buckles.
4. Check girth straps on saddles for cracks and splits.
5. Check every part of reins (especially where they are attached to the bit) for cracks and bend them both ways. Try to tear them in half – you should not be able to but often can.
6. Check bits for sharp edges.
7. Check nickel bits for bends and cracks.
8. Check stirrup irons for bends and cracks and discourage the use of nickel for bits and stirrup irons.
9. Check safety stirrup irons for bending and "opening up". When "opened up" they can break. When "opened up" the rider's foot is at an angle so that more weight is put over their little toe.
10. Check all stitching.

Teaching new pupils

All riders may fall off when learning to ride but many falls could be avoided if instructors foresaw dangers and did not ask of pupils too much too soon.

Find out from new pupils what previous riding experience they have had. Watch them to see if they sit in a relaxed position and have light even contact on the reins. (A rider tipping forward and clutching onto over-tight, over-short reins is a clear indication that he or she is very frightened and must be taught very slowly and carefully.)

Sitting trot
Unless riders can sit correctly, easily, comfortably and safely in sitting trot with their stirrups do not try them without stirrups. They are likely to fall off because without stirrups they will start to lose their balance and slip sideways especially on corners.

In trot once this sideways slip has started it will progress until they fall off.

Canter
Cantering round a school is much more difficult than cantering in a straight line.

Riders learning to canter tend to lose their balance on corners and slip off to the outside because their weight has gone over more into their outside stirrup and outside seat bone.

1. Try to teach canter on the long, straight side of the school only, trotting before and after the canter. School horses should answer to *your* voice asking them for canter then for trot again.
2. Coming back to trot after canter is also a dodgy moment for beginners and as this is likely to coincide with a corner they must be warned to sit more onto their inside seat bone before and during corners.
3. Do not try to teach canter until pupils can ride at sitting trot correctly, easily and safely without stirrups and guide their horse accurately while doing so. Hurrying the teaching of canter before pupils are ready for it is the cause of many falls.
4. If a pupil is doubtful of their ability to do something or says that they are frightened, do not ask them to do it. Someone lacking in confidence is likely to stiffen with fright, so will easily become unbalanced and be likely to fall off.
5. Older or disabled riders are likely to tire more easily so don't make the second half of the lesson too demanding.
6. Even experienced riders will get very tired if they have not ridden for

several years. Their balance and coordination may be disappointingly bad after a long gap with no riding. Don't expect too much of them.

Teaching jumping

The horse to be used for teaching jumping must go quietly and smoothly, go straight and jump in its stride. You cannot safely teach jumping on a horse which rushes at a jump flat out nor on one which refuses or runs out. Using such horses for teaching jumping is asking for trouble. So is asking pupils to jump before they are sufficiently experienced, balanced and confident.

A rider who does not want to jump should not be made or encouraged to do so. Not wanting to go over a jump tends to make a rider sit back, stiffen and brace against their stirrups – all things which will almost guarantee that they will not "go with" the horse as it jumps and so will be thrown up in the air and almost certainly fall off. They will be far more apprehensive and therefore even more likely to fall off next time.

To be successful, happy and confident when jumping, riders must *want* to jump and it is up to you, the instructor, not to try to teach them to jump until they really are ready and capable of doing so. It is also up to you to see that they make progress slowly and as safely as possible so that they do not lose confidence by having an unnecessary fall through your lack of care and judgement regarding the ability of horse and rider.

Common causes of falls

1. Sudden sideways movements. Don't put a very novice or very nervous pupil on an animal which shies sideways, or on a horse which is frightened of other horses near it and will jink sideways away from them.
2. Stopping or starting suddenly. Pupils are likely to fall off if a horse canters nearly up to the heels of the horse in front then stops suddenly. The rider may go on and will fall off onto or very near the heels of the horse in front.
3. Jumping. There is absolutely no point in trying to teach anyone to jump until they are really safe, stable and confident in the saddle at all gaits.

They need to be able to canter happily with a shorter stirrup and their seat out of the saddle without any swaying or lurching.

Falls out on a hack

Do not take riders out on hacks unless you know that they are happy and can control their horse at all gaits to be used on the hack. This may involve a few minutes' trial in a small enclosed area where you can watch the rider and assess their ability.

You cannot take people at their word when they say, "I am very experienced. I have been riding for eight years." They may only have been on a nose to trail trek a few times each year. Asking for a fast or lively horse is often an indication of lack of knowledge or experience.

The way an unknown rider dresses and the way they approach a horse tells you a certain amount. What they check before they mount, how they mount and what they check or adjust for themselves after they mount tell you a lot. Nothing tells you as much as actually seeing them out on a hack during which you intend to canter.

Falls on hacks can be caused by:
1. A horse shying or stumbling.
2. A horse kicking out at another.
3. A horse moving quickly to avoid being kicked.
4. Sudden swerves.
5. The rider catching their leg on gateways or trees.
6. A horse getting left behind and going fast to catch up, perhaps slowing down very suddenly when it has caught up.
7. Going too fast downhill.
8. Not being able to control the horse at canter.
9. A rider trying to hold their horse back when the others canter because they do not want to canter. This is a common cause of real accidents. The escort is perhaps unaware that one rider is frightened and does not want to canter. That rider tries to hold their horse back and prevent it cantering with the others. The normal behaviour of a horse under these circumstances is either to reach and dive to try to get its head or to leap or buck. It will be determined to go on with its friends so will take con-

trol and may go very fast indeed to catch up with the others. Its excitement and speed may even take it on past the others and it may continue to go very fast particularly if it is going towards home.

Many very serious accidents have been caused in exactly the ways I have described above. The escort must be aware if someone does not want to canter. Even if they appear to have cantered happily once or twice already they may have felt frightened and not want to canter a third time. People are very loathe to admit that they are frightened; they can be reluctant and slow to speak up and voice their feelings. The escort must be certain every time that *all* the riders do want another canter. If someone has doubts they must not be put in the position where they *have* to – their horse taking them off following the others in canter.

To stay on a horse at different gaits and over varying terrain, to cope with unexpected sudden movements of the horse, to avoid holes and bushes and to control a horse that is wanting to go on and is much stronger and keener than it would be in a lesson in an enclosed area, needs a fairly skilful rider and one with a lot of confidence.

Riders are probably more likely to fall off on a hack than during a lesson on the flat. Even so, if a rider had two falls on one hack I would think that they were not sufficiently experienced to be out on a hack, their horse was too much for them or the pace chosen or the terrain chosen was unsuitable for that rider's ability.

The pace and the choice of ground should be geared to the least able rider. Ideally, riders of different ability should be on separate hacks. Where this applies, a rider is not put in the embarrassing position of feeling that, by saying that they do not want to canter, they are spoiling the ride for the others.

An experienced person with a knowledge and understanding of horses and people and who can foresee danger must be in charge. They must know the ability of each rider and the peculiarities of each horse. They must be aware that on a cold windy day and after a few days off or in a certain area a horse can behave out of character – and notice if one is doing so and re-plan the ride accordingly.

If there are more than six people there should be two escorts. A leading rein should be carried by the escort who should be riding a quiet, sensible horse from which they are able to lead another horse if necessary.

Dealing with falls

A fall is frightening. Even if the rider is completely unhurt they can be severely shocked and can feel shaky and disorientated.

Make absolutely certain that they are unhurt, can remember what happened and are talking sense before asking them to remount. If they don't want to do so don't force them – give them time. Don't expect them to repeat whatever made them fall off; ask for something much, much easier to regain their confidence. If there is any possibility of even slight concussion do not allow the rider to remount.

Think carefully about why they fell off. Did the horse's behaviour cause the fall? Do you now realise that what you were asking them to do might have been in any way a bit too difficult for them? Could your over-high expectations of them have caused the fall?

If someone has, for any reason, fallen off in your lesson it is absolutely essential to do everything you possibly can to ensure that they do not have a second fall in the same lesson.

When a rider has had a fall in a lesson I think that whoever takes them in their next lesson should not only know that they had a fall last time but should also know how that fall happened. They can then avoid the circumstances and try to regain that rider's confidence.

Sensible safety precautions

1. Do not canter towards home when hacking out.
2. Walk from the lesson area to the stables.
3. Lead any animal which has a tendency to rush to the stables and therefore might be too much for its rider once it is outside the enclosed teaching area.
4. Be very aware of those horses which are bored or those which are very quiet and lazy to ride in the school, but become strong, keen lively characters when in an open field.

5. If someone does fall off do not let them remount unless you are 100 per cent sure that: you saw them fall; that the fall was only a gentle one; and that nothing hurts.
6. Remember that, even if a rider lands on his or her feet and is quite obviously unhurt, a report must still go into the Accident Book.
7. If in doubt do not move the rider. Get help.
8. Keep the rest of the ride at halt, well away from the fallen rider.
9. Do not give the fallen rider anything to drink.
10. Remember how the fall occurred. Ask others if they saw what happened and if they were involved. Write it all down in the Accident Book in detail as soon as possible.

Teaching dismounted

Having something for the pupils to look at and examine is a tremendous help in teaching because:
1. It creates interest.
2. The image of what you show sticks in their memories better than words.

It is also a good idea to collect:
1. Different types of bits.
2. The bones of a foreleg.
3. The skull and top and bottom jaws with teeth. (2 and 3 can be easily obtained from hunt kennels and from some slaughterhouses.)
4. Small bags of horse food of identical weight but surprisingly different sizes – for example, 1 kilo bran, 1 kilo nuts.
5. Haynets of different exact weights of hay.
6. Good and bad samples of meadow hay and seed hay.
7. Samples of wheat, oat and barley straw.
8. Wood chips, sawdust, peat, paper bedding samples.
9. Cut out pictures showing good and bad conformation stuck on a sheet of cardboard.
10. Cut out positions of good and bad riding and jumping positions.
11. Shoes of as many types as possible.

12. The syllabus for BHS exams you may be asked to help pupils with.
13. The syllabus for riding club exams.
14. Have all the Pony Club Test Cards and if you have a ride at Pony Club camp find out which tests they are going to take – try to teach them everything on that card.
15. Keep up to date with riding and road safety test requirements and know exactly how pupils should be prepared for this test.
16. For Pony Club camps or courses of several days' duration plan competitions for the next day which will test what has been remembered from today's lesson.
17. With a sufficiently large and varied collection of numbered objects a competition involving the entire camp can be fairly easily set up.

These are just a few ideas as a foundation for you to build on.

Dangers on foot

1. Do not tie horses up just inside or just outside a stable doorway. If they try to go through, the rope will jerk their heads sideways, their bodies will bend double and they may fall and get cast in the doorway.
2. Do not let anyone muck out with a horse loose in the stable or a barrow across the doorway. If the horse barges out past the barrow the horse or the person mucking out in the doorway can be badly hurt.
3. Tie haynets really high. Pass the cord through the bottom of the net before pulling the bottom up high towards the top so that, when empty, the net will hang in a U-shape well clear of the ground. If it hangs too low, a horse could get its leg caught in it.
4. Never let small children go into a field or stable with loose horses. A playful young horse in a field or stable may strike out with a foreleg and kill a child. Two jealous horses in a field trying to kick each other can kick and hurt or kill a child.

Accident book

Remember that every fall or accident of any sort, even a rider's foot being trodden on while beside the horse, must be recorded in the Accident Book in full detail.

At one time or another, some of your pupils are going to fall off but do try to avoid this happening by being very observant and noticing if:
1. A horse is more lively than usual.
2. A rider is not riding as well as usual.
3. A rider seems more nervous than usual.
d. There are unusual noises or comings and goings in the yard which may disturb some horses.
4. It is a cold windy day when nearly all horses are more alert and jumpy.
5. There is a new horse or new horses in the ride.
6. There are pupils new to you in the ride.
7. One of the riders fell off last time. I think it is *very* important that instructors should know of this, as it is part of their job to make as sure as is possible that this rider does not have another fall in their lesson.
8. A rider seems unhappy, nervous or worried on a particular horse. If this is the case, and if possible, change them on to another horse.

You should change the lesson plan if what you were going to ask the ride to do is probably beyond the capability of someone in your ride. Also take the time and trouble to lower or completely alter jumps if a horse or rider has lost confidence. If someone actually asks to change horses, or before mounting says that they do not want to ride a particular horse really try to do as they wish. Always check that:
1. Jumps are built safely.
2. Jump cups not in use are removed.
3. Girths are tight enough.
4. There is nothing hard or dangerous to fall on in the ground line of the fence or at the bottom of jump stands – for example, milk crates or a pile of bricks.

3 The rider's position in the saddle

The pelvis that a rider sits on

I believe that imagining and "pretending" are very much part of teaching because through them you can enable a rider to visualise and, most important, *feel* a way of riding.

How a rider sits in the saddle and what part of their pelvis supports their weight are all important. Most riders have no idea what the part of their pelvis that they sit on looks like. Very few instructors know or have given the subject the thought and study that this vital part of a rider deserves. Experimenting with your own pelvic position and changing your weight while sitting on a stool is a real eye opener.

On a stool of suitable height, and sitting in riding position, imagine yourself to be teaching and carry out the corrections for position that you might give to a rider. You may be amazed to find that some of your corrections do not work, some are positively harmful and some are "spot on".

You *must* try out what you teach on yourself and see if the feel is good, bad or indifferent. I am sure that there must have been times as a pupil or student when you have been told to do something in riding which you have felt made you worse. It is quite probable that the person teaching had never experimented on themselves to see if what they taught you made sense and worked for a rider. It is up to you to make sure that you think, feel and try things out yourself to make sure that you do not mislead your pupils.

We talk about sitting on our seat bones which many people visualise as two points sticking out at the bottom of the pelvis. The "tail" end of the

Pelvis: seat bones. Sitting on the "back" seat bones (left): *"Sit on your bottom and ride your horse forward." Good. Sitting on the "front" seat bones* (centre): *rider tipping forward, weak and ineffective. Bracing the back* (right): *extra use of the "back" two seat bones to make the rider stronger and more effective. Good.*

spine, the coccyx, is at the centre back of the pelvis and should not come into contact with the saddle. We sit on the two curved areas of bone at each side of the pelvis. These bones have a slightly flattened surface area about 2.5cm (1in) wide and about 10.2–15.2cm (4–6in) long. Our weight can be taken anywhere on this length on each side of the pelvis but we are only in contact with one area on each side at a time. We are balancing on a total of two very small areas so it is all a bit precarious.

If you change the weight-bearing areas of your pelvis and move them further forward by just 5.1cm, by bringing your shoulders further forward you may feel unbalanced, insecure and as if you are tipping forward and going to fall off forwards. That *minute* altering of the weight-bearing area, just moving it 5cm (2in) forward, has made a major difference to your feeling of stability and security in the saddle. Riding with your stirrups one hole too long has the same effect.

Riding in a deep-seated saddle which is too short for you so that you are sitting with an uphill slope under your bottom behind you has the same effect as does sitting in a saddle which is lower in front than behind.

Sitting on a horse which is higher in the hindquarters than at the withers can put you in this position. A nervous beginner who leans forward and clutches will put themselves in this position. Someone riding with very short reins will pull themselves forward into this position.

I know that we have *not* got four seat bones – two on each side – but it is a great help in teaching if you can get your pupils to pretend that they have four seat bones – two "back" ones and two "front" ones.

All the descriptions above visualise a rider allowing his or her own weight to roll forward along the bearing surface of their pelvis until it is being taken on their imaginary two "front" seat bones. Try to find out why this has occurred. If it is because the stirrups are too long, try them one or two holes shorter; look at the result and ask the rider if they can now feel that their weight is on or nearer to their two "back" seat bones.

If the rider is sitting on an uphill slope at the back of the saddle ask them to sit further forward in the saddle, or if the saddle is obviously much too short for the rider try to change it for a longer saddle. Many young horses become higher behind than in front at some point in their growth. If ridden at this stage they can become very unbalanced and "on their forehand". They are also uncomfortable to ride as they throw the rider forward on to their two "front" seat bones. Some older horses are simply built this way and this makes learning to ride on them more difficult for the novice rider.

The nervous beginner and "over shortener" of the reins can be helped by fixing coloured elastic bands at the correct length for holding the reins so that the rider can sit upright more easily and will not be pulled forward because they have their hands so far forward along the horse's neck.

All riders should be helped to sit on their two "back" seat bones. There are so many times when all the instructor need say to a rider is, "Sit on your bottom, sit on your back two seat bones and ride your horse forward."

For instance:
1. When a horse spooks at something.
2. When a horse is being lazy.
3. When a horse is humping its back and threatening to buck.
4. When it is threatening to kick another horse.

5. When it is cutting corners.
6. When it is trying to go sideways.
7. When it doesn't want to pass another horse.
8. When it doesn't want to leave the stable yard.
9. When it doesn't want to turn away from home.
10. When you are teaching someone to get a horse on the bit.
11. Between jumps when you are teaching someone to ride a course.
12. Riding on a loose or long rein.
13. Teaching riders sitting trot.
14. Asking for canter.

There are endless occasions where that very simple instruction gives the rider the action and feel necessary to obtain control or the required result from the horse.

Sitting on their "front" two seat bones makes riders wobbly, tippy and ineffective in their riding. Two "front" seat bones and two "back" seat bones are easy for riders to visualise and can be used when teaching all levels – from a tiny child beginner to an advanced rider. It really does feel as if your weight can move from the two "front" seat bones to the two "back" ones. Try it yourself and see if you agree. Purists may criticise you for teaching in this way but I know that it works better and more quickly than any other way and as riders find it easy to understand I feel it cannot be a bad way of teaching. If it works do it. I hope that you will try it yourself in your teaching and find out how quickly it is successful.

Saddles and position

It is very difficult to improve pupils' positions if they are sitting in saddles which put them in the wrong place.

The commonest fault is saddles which sit up too high in front and make the rider's seat slip backwards so that they sit in the lowest point – far too near the back of the saddle. This position can make them sit with their legs stuck forward so that they are always out of balance with the horse, completely behind the movement and in an impossible position from which to rise to the trot comfortably.

The rider's position in the saddle 23

Saddles. This saddle (above) will make the rider slip to the lowest point. When this happens the rider will sit like this (below).

When a temporary correction is made, by inserting stuffing under the back end of the saddle (above) the rider will find it easy to sit naturally like this (below). If this sort of stuffing will not do the trick, then change the saddle

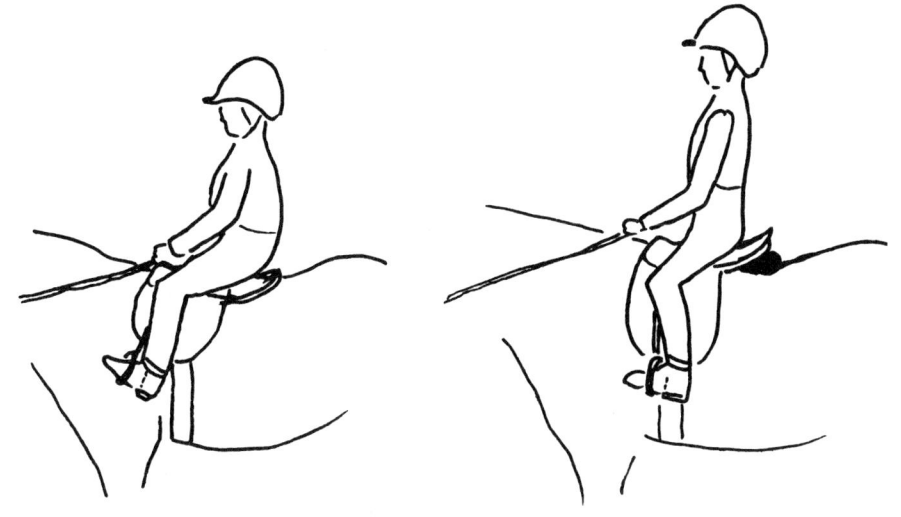

The rider should be sitting in balance over their feet. In whatever gait they are riding if the horse was magically whisked from under them they should land in balance on their feet. The rider who has slid to the back of a saddle cocked up high in front, legs sticking forward, would land heavily on their bottom.

Get your eye in so that you can recognise a rider who is sitting in balance over their feet and learn to spot one who is even slightly behind the

Saddles. A saddle with a flat seat (top) *gives the rider no support. A good, well-shaped saddle* (centre) *provides a safe and comfortable ride. A saddle which is higher in front and slopes to the back will cause the rider's seat to slide towards the back of the saddle and the rider's legs will tend to stick out in front.*

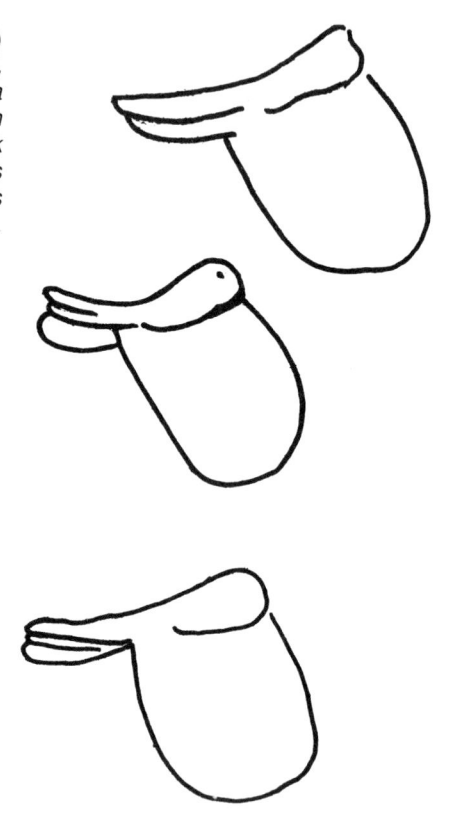

movement, either because they are leaning back slightly or because their legs are a little too far forward. Check their saddles to see that they are sitting level on the horse without even a slight backward slope. It is useful to carry some pieces of foam which can temporarily lift the back of the saddle if they are inserted between the saddle and a numnah.

It is no good saying, "Put your lower leg further back and sit up tall." The riders' legs are not the cause of the problem (although the leg position shows it up most) – it is their seat.

You must say, "Sit further forward in the saddle," and if necessary tell them to put one hand on the front of the saddle to help them stay forward. Then say, "Put your lower legs back; think of keeling; bend your knees; think of your knees as headlights, they must be in front of you to light the way." Any simple words which convey what you want riders to do and which they can picture in their minds will help. For children or adults it is much better to keep things simple instead of using technical jargon.

If the saddle on quite a wide, fat horse is coming down on its withers suspect a broken tree. To test for this take the saddle off the horse and hold the back of the saddle against your stomach, seat upwards. Put one hand round each side of the front of the saddle just above where the "point pocket" holds and protects the end of the tree. When you try to bend the saddle in both directions, see if there is any movement between your two hands or if there are any "squeaking" sounds in that part. A broken-treed saddle should not be used. It is unsafe and can damage the horse's back. Some can be mended with a metal plate but they often "go" again.

If the saddle is continually sliding up the neck of a fat little pony without much shoulder, its saddle can be fitted with point straps. These are two extra girth straps fitted one on each side to the point of the saddle tree where the ends are protected by two little leather pockets. These two extra straps have the effect of anchoring the front of the saddle down and stopping it slipping forward. Obviously, if this is to work the saddle must be a reasonable fit on the pony in the first place. Attach the girth to the two new girth straps and the ones next to them. If when girthed like this the back of the saddle moves up and down use the new straps and the next but one girth strap. This system is preferable to a crupper which is ugly and can be very uncomfortable for the pony when it rounds its back to jump.

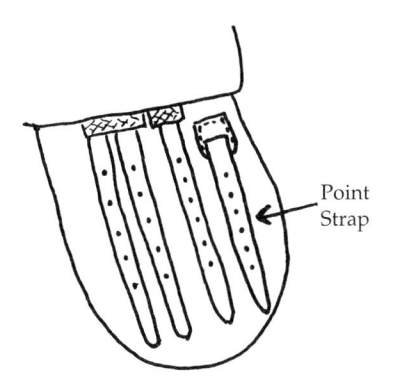

A point strap (arrowed)

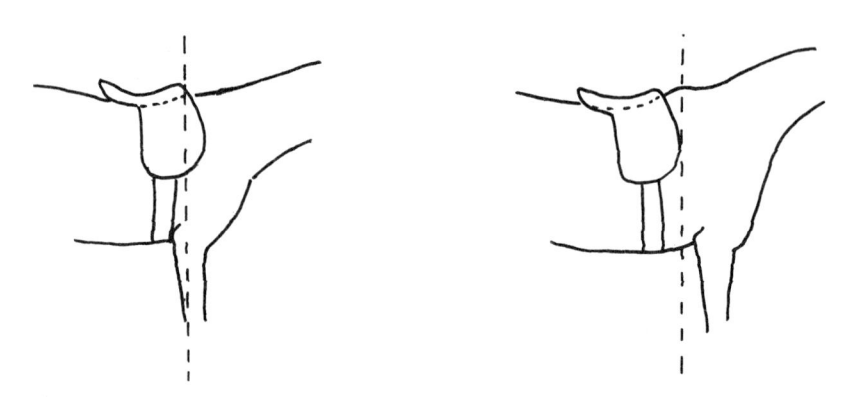

Straight shoulder. This saddle (left) sits too far forward. The imaginary line from the highest point of the wither to the ground goes down the foreleg. This saddle will slip up the horse's neck, though a point strap may help prevent this. A saddle (right) which sits back behind the shoulder. The good line from the highest point of the wither to the ground, is positioned well behind the foreleg.

If a saddle is continually slipping back, look at the horse's shape behind the girth. Normally, a horse's stomach bulges down behind the girth so that the girth is naturally held forward in place. Some horses, probably rather lean ones, have a very definite uphill slope behind the girth. They are described as "herring gutted". In a horse of this type first the girth slips back, then the saddle goes too.

If the problem is only slight a martingale is often sufficient to hold the girth in place. If this will not work the horse must have a breastplate. This is a leather neckstrap with small straps which attach to "Ds" at the front of

A "herring gutted" horse where the uphill slope behind the elbow allows the girth to slip back, followed by the saddle.

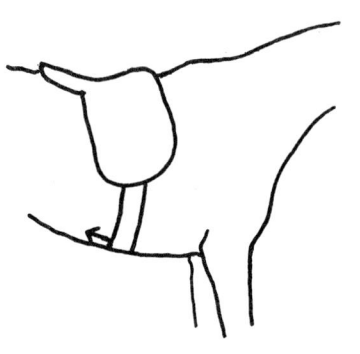

The rider's position in the saddle

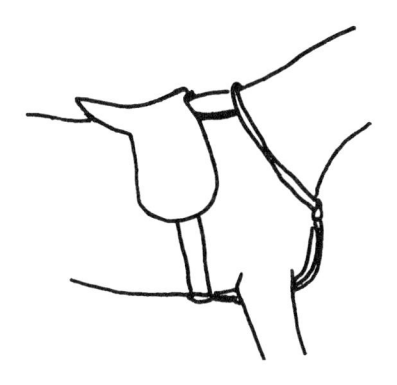

The breast plate helps to keep the saddle forward and in the correct position.

the saddle on each side of the withers. Another strap goes from the bottom of the neckstrap onto the girth between the forelegs. It must be adjusted so that it keeps the girth forward but does not interfere with the horse's freedom of movement by being too tight in front of its shoulders.

A breast girth can also help to keep a saddle forward. This is a wide leather or webbing strap which goes round the front of the horse's chest

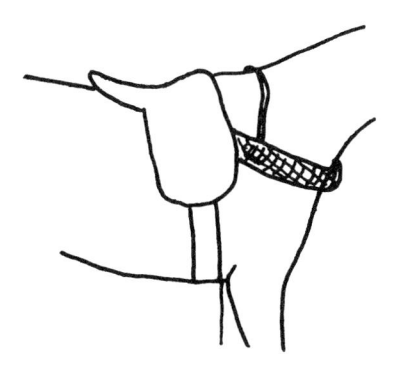

The breast girth help keeps the saddle in the correct forward position.

and is attached at each side to the girth or girth straps by adjustable leather straps. A narrow adjustable piece of leather goes over the withers to keep the breast girth up and to regulate its height. A wrongly adjusted breast girth can press on the horse's windpipe if it is set too high and interfere with its shoulder action if set too low.

4 The conformation of the rider

Riders come in many shapes and sizes. Two riders of the same height and weight can have very different proportions, one very long backed, one very short. One with long arms, one with short. Another with flat lean thighs, the next with short fat ones. Some people are naturally round shouldered perhaps also with necks and heads poking forward and probably collapsed and rounded backs, others naturally stand and walk hollow backed with their bottoms sticking out. Some people naturally stand and walk with toes turned in, for others "toes out" comes naturally. Some people sit, stand and walk very crooked, one shoulder lower than the other, spine twisted, perhaps head tilted to one side.

It is your job as an instructor to notice this and work out the problems

Some riders sit on a horse crooked

that physical differences may present for each rider and how you can overcome them. You must realise that an exercise which will help one rider in your class may actually make another rider worse by accentuating their fault. It is up to you to choose an alternative exercise for that rider.

Short back

The short-backed rider has a lower centre of gravity so they are likely to find it easier to keep their balance on a horse. A short back in a person (as in a horse) is usually strong and more likely to be trouble free.

Long back

A long-backed person tends to be less stable on a horse partly because their centre of gravity is higher and partly because they have a longer area of back to control. This is especially true if they are very thin and lack muscle. They are more likely to lose their balance forwards, backwards or sideways.

Long legs, lean flat thighs

A good length of leg helps to stabilise the upper body and enables the rider to use their legs effectively on a large horse. Flat thighs help the rider to sit close to the horse and be part of it. A rider so made is likely to find it easier to stay on a difficult horse. It will also be a great deal easier to mount from the ground.

Short legs, round thighs

People with short legs and round thighs tend to look and feel as if they are perched, somewhat precariously, on top of the horse as opposed to sitting deep into it.

Round thighs can allow the rider's leg to roll out of place so that the back of the thigh comes onto the saddle, the knee comes right away from the saddle, the back of the calf comes onto the horse's sides and is used to grip, the toes turn out and the heels press into the horse's sides for extra grip. The rider appears to be clinging on with their legs for dear life and the horse, feeling the pressure of the rider's calves and heels, may interpret them as aids to go faster (sometimes much faster, causing the rider to grip and press more strongly still, upon which the horse increases pace even more) the last thing that this rider wants.

To help such a rider, start the correction at the top of the leg at the ball and socket joint of the hip. Ask them to lift, say, their left seat bone and put it down as far away from their right seat bone as possible, then lift their right seat bone and put it down as far away from their left seat bone as possible. This, besides getting them to sit deeper in the saddle, will slightly alter the angle of their leg so that the inside of the thigh will be on the saddle more. Now, as they are sitting upright, ask them with their left hand to lift their left thigh muscle out behind their leg and pull it further back, repeating the action with the right side. This will help to keep the thighs in a flatter position in the saddle which will bring the knees closer to the saddle, make calf grip less likely and bring the toes in more towards the horse's sides without stiffening the rider. This must all be done gently by the rider – and you must not pull, push or twist the rider's joints.

People with fat rounded thighs are often more stable and more effective if they ride with their stirrups one hole shorter than you might expect from other riders.

Remember that it is often very difficult for people with short legs and round thighs to mount. Be ready to help before they feel awkward and have to ask.

Short arms

One disadvantage of short arms is that they limit the possibilities of the angle between the rider's upper arm and the line of forearm, wrist, hand, rein to horse's mouth. Short arms also limit the amount of extra rein the rider can give the horse when they push their hands forward towards the horse's mouth, without actually altering the length of their reins. It is also very difficult for the rider with short arms to lower their hands without tipping forward when riding a horse with a very low head carriage. They will naturally have to carry their hands a little higher to enable them to sit upright and in balance.

Long arms

Long arms are versatile as to the height at which the rider carries their hands. There is no problem here. People with long arms tend to try to gain more control by bringing their hands back towards their body instead of shortening the reins. This action can bring their elbows back behind their body line and cause them to lean their body back behind their hands and so sit very much behind the movement. Their lower legs and feet may come forward and the rider may press against the stirrups at the same time so pushing themselves further back in the saddle.

The easiest way to bring this rider forward and into balance with the horse is to say, "Shorten your rein." And, "Shorten them more and then

The correct position of the hands for the rider with short arms and (dotted line) *the rider with long arms.*

some more," until their upper body has come forward into an upright position. Coloured elastic bands on the reins are the quickest way of helping this rider to keep their reins short enough so that their upper arm does not go back behind the vertical angle of their body. They will then get the feel of going forward in balance with the horse instead of being constantly behind the movement.

Overweight

Problems are caused for both horse and rider where the rider is overweight. An overweight rider is less stable, being top heavy, and will find it more difficult to keep his or her balance.

The constant change of balance of the rider's considerable weight is going to make it more difficult, and therefore more tiring, for a horse to carry them.

Overweight riders are likely to be less fit than slimmer riders and will therefore tire more quickly. They are likely to fall more easily and may land heavily and awkwardly. There is not much you can do unless you dare to tactfully suggest that they would find riding easier and make more progress if they lost weight!

Round shoulders

People who sit and walk round shouldered are not going to find it easy to sit up straight on a horse. Why should they improve if they only sit up straight when they ride for an hour a day or an hour a week, when they spend the rest of their time slumped in a chair or slouching along in a round-shouldered walk? Encourage them to hold themselves upright between lessons to strengthen their muscles and get the feel of being taller and better balanced on their own feet.

Looking down can start the problem if it becomes a constant habit. The weight of the rider's head then pulls their neck and shoulders forward. These, now rounded shoulders often cause a collapsed back.

If riders walk and sit round shouldered when not on a horse they will not improve with just one hour's correction daily or perhaps only weekly

The conformation of the rider

when riding. To improve their riding they must correct their own posture when not on a horse.

Collapsed back

A collapsed back can be very obvious and is very frequently seen at walk. The rider's head, neck and shoulders poke forward, forward, forward to the rhythm of the horse's walk and at the same time the stomach and the small of the back (waistline) move back, back, back.

Some riders with a collapsed back swing their forward-tilted shoulders left, right, left, right in rhythm with the horse's walk.

Collapsed back is often accompanied by round shoulders. Their shoulders collapse forward and their back collapses to the rear

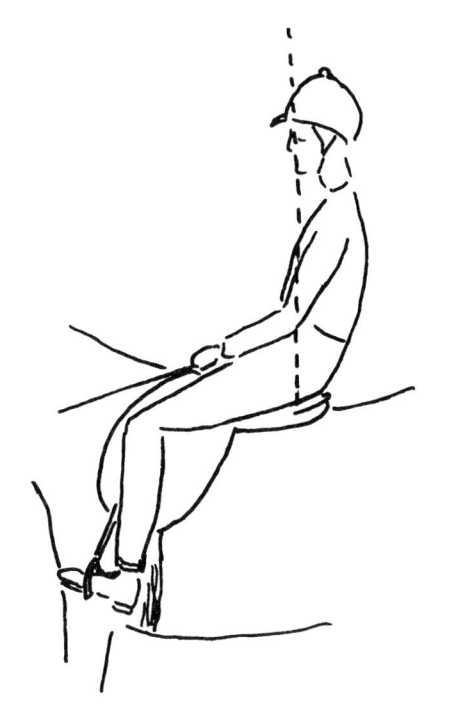

Collapsed back: the rider is leaning backwards, out of balance.

34   Teaching Riding

A rider whose position indicates a collapsed back; note the accompanying faults of toes down and round shoulders.

The problem may have started in the back and led to round shoulders and head poking forward.

Symptoms of collapsed back
1. The pelvis is often tilted at a wrong angle, too far backwards.
2. The rider is sitting with their weight too far back on their bottom.
3. Their coccyx (tail bone) is tucked in underneath them far too much.
4. The waistband of their jods is too far down near to the back of the saddle.

Tell them to think, "Push the two front points of your pelvis forward. Now take a deep breath and sit tall, then lean back a little above your waist."

Head and neck poking forward

Collapsed back and round shoulders are often accompanied by head and neck poking forwards, a continuation of the "question mark" shape. All of these last three problems can be corrected in much the same way.

Try not to say, "Sit up straight," as this is likely to make riders stiffen. Instead, ask them to, "Take a big breath and fill your lungs as full as possible with air." If they fill their lungs with air the air "pumps them up" into an upright position without any stiffening. Now tell them to imagine that they have got to shout up over the top of a high building to make someone on the other side hear them. They will need to re-fill their lungs with air, look up, tilt their head up and back and lift their chin to throw their voice up and over. They should now quite naturally be sitting upright and in balance without having strained or stiffened to attain this position.

At walk, ask them to put both reins in a bridge in their outside hand and their inside hand in the small of their back, palm outwards. (Do this exercise with the reins in the outside hand so that the rider's outside shoulder is a little forward of their inside shoulder and therefore at the same angle as their horse's shoulders.) Ask them to imagine the hand in their back is the back of a bench – and ask them to lean back slightly over the back of the "bench".

At walk, both round shouldered and collapsed back riders tend to follow the movement of the horse's walk with their bodies; they move the small of their back outwards towards the horse's tail and nod their heads forwards. Their hand in the small of their back will help to correct this if you say, "Now you should be able to feel your stomach coming forward, forward, forward to absorb the rhythm of the horse's walk."

To help this rider sit up tall, without stiffening, the instructor has asked him to take a big breath and put his hand in the small of his back, palm outwards. This position allows the rider's back to straighten and his stomach to come forward naturally.

Reins in a "bridge", held in one hand.

Right hand in the small of the back, with palm outwards. This rider is practising the exercise to correct a collapsed back.

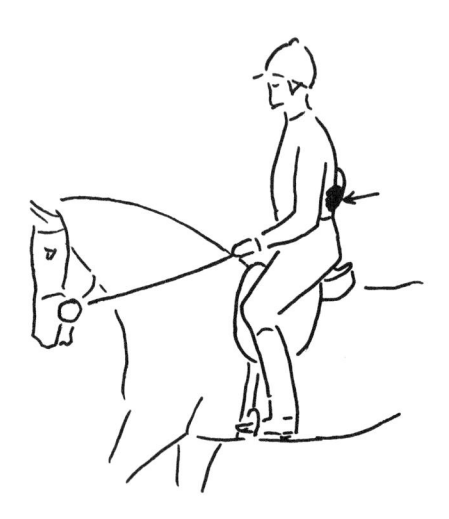

Concentrate your attention on one person until he or she has got the movement correct. The change in their position should by now be very obvious so encourage the other riders to look at this one rider and speak out if they can see the difference. This makes the rider feel good and also makes all the other riders aware of how their own backs should move at walk. If there really is the big difference that there should be it helps to give the whole ride confidence in you as a teacher.

Work the exercise of hand in the small of the back on both reins. It is something everyone in the ride will benefit from with the exception of the hollow-backed, bottom-sticking-out rider. It will only make them worse.

Two other ways of suggesting the position you want them to be in are to tell them that they are a puppet on a string and the string is pulling their head up higher and higher. First, they try to see over the head of the rider in front of them and, second, they try to grow tall slowly, then taller and taller.

Don't forget to tell riders how much more elegant and, if applicable, slimmer they look when sitting tall and upright!

Some, otherwise elegant, riders develop the habit of poking their necks and heads forward while keeping their backs fairly straight when they are schooling their horses or riding a dressage test. They use this ugly way of riding when they are working hard trying to ride their horse forward strongly with their seat and legs. Their bobbing head in sitting trot looks like an agitated hen. At walk and canter they look more like tortoises!

It is not only ugly, it makes them less effective riders. Many have absolutely no idea that they have developed this habit.

A demonstration of how they look done laughingly – not cruelly – can really make them think but you must know your rider before you imitate them. You must never make one of your pupils feel a fool.

Continue with the same exercise of hand in the small of the back in sitting trot, in canter and in transitions up from halt to canter and down if the rider is capable of doing this.

Watch out for riders who are by now tending to go hollow backed and let them ride normally again.

Hollow back

People who sit and walk hollow backed usually have their bottoms sticking out behind and may also have their tummies sticking out in front to compensate and balance their body. They are likely also to ride in this position.

Collapsed back and hollow back are two completely opposite faults and may be seen in two different riders in the same class. This is a typical example of where an exercise to improve one rider will actually make the other rider worse.

Instructors must not just "do" an exercise with everyone in the class without noticing riders' different problems and changing or slightly altering the exercise to suit individual riders.

Discuss the problem and point out that many hours per day are spent sitting, standing or walking and perhaps only one hour a day or even one hour a week is spent riding. The hollow back will not alter unless the rider is aware of it nearly all the time and tries to correct their own posture every day when they are not on a horse. There are several helpful thoughts and exercises to use while on a horse. "Tuck your tummy in." "Tuck your bottom in underneath you." "Try to get the waistband at the back of your jods/breeches closer to the back of your saddle.

At halt, ask the riders to take their feet out of their stirrups, and to sit as far forward in the saddle as possible and slowly bend their knees until they are touching above the horse's withers. This action will straighten their back naturally. Ask them to think about the different position in which they are now sitting on their back seat bones (their weight is now taken further back on their pelvis) and to keep that new feel as they slowly lower both legs.

You must watch their back very carefully as they lower their legs and stop them as soon as you think they will start to become slightly hollow backed again if they go lower still with their legs. Readjust their stirrup leathers because they will probably now be riding one or two holes shorter. It does not matter one bit if they now look as if they are riding at jumping length. The shorter stirrup puts them further back on their seat bones just as the knee raising exercise did. Shorter stirrups make it far easier for riders to correct their position, lose their hollow back and get the habit of sitting correctly. Only when you are sure that they can still hold their better position effortlessly must you drop their leathers a hole. Do not try to get them to ride with long stirrups. Just one hole too long can

Practising position. Hollow back (left), *bottom and stomach sticking out. Knees* (centre) *are drawn up to touch above the withers so that the rider's seat contact with the saddle is in the correct place. Hand* (right) *on the rider's stomach to tuck it in.*

allow their weight to roll further forward on their pelvis and onto their front seat bones. They will then revert to a hollow-back, bottom-sticking-out position. This is often described as "sitting on their fork".

Collapsed hip, sitting crooked

A rider may sit crooked on a horse because they habitually stand, sit on a chair and walk crooked. An old leg or hip injury may have caused them to change their balance to ease the pain. They can be trying to ease spinal or muscular back pain by altering their position or they may have been born with a spinal deformity or with one leg longer than the other. (This is quite a common problem.)

Before making corrections or doing exercises make sure, tactfully, that there is no history of back problems which you could aggravate.

During a lesson always spend some time standing directly behind riders so that you can see if they are sitting straight or crooked. Standing in a corner facing down the long side of the school is a good place to watch from. Also watch your ride from the outside of a circle to see if they are slipping to the outside as they ride round.

A rider sitting crooked. Best seen by the instructor if he or she stands behind the ride and watches each pupil as they go away. In a corner of the school facing down the long side is a good place from which to assess the ride.

The signs to look for in a rider are easiest seen from behind them.
1. One shoulder lower than the other. (Usually the inside one.)
2. The rider sitting over more to the outside of the saddle.
3. The heel of the inside leg coming up (because their seat has slipped across to the outside of the saddle).
4. Collapsed inside hip. (Rider appears to be bent inwards over the hip.)
5. Head tilted to the inside.
6. Spine curved.
7. Centre seam of coat crooked.

Stand behind the ride and on the outside of the circle to check these faults. Nearly all riders will sit crooked to the outside on a circle in one direction. This often goes unspotted because the instructor spends most of his or her time looking out at the ride from inside. For this reason it is essential during a lesson to see the riders on both reins from the outside.

Position yourself behind them as they ride on a circle away from you and stand tight up in a corner so that you can see their back view as they ride in a straight line. Possible suggestions to put to them are:
1. "Lengthen the inside of your body, making your inside ear and your inside heel as far away from each other as possible." This puts more weight onto their inside seat bone. (By slipping sideways to the outside they are putting more weight on their outside seat bone.)
2. An "opposite" suggestion could be, "Take a big breath and really fill your lungs with air. Now think of getting your outside ear closer to your outside hip." (The big breath is necessary first or they may just crumple up.)

In teaching it is very necessary to use at least two different wordings or methods of correction because what works in the mind of one rider does not necessarily work for another.

Toes out

If a rider's natural stance and way of walking is "toes out" they are going to ride toe out. This problem needs tackling carefully because it originates in the ball and socket hip joint. The angle at which the ball fits into the socket controls the natural position of a person's feet. Lift one foot off the ground and put your hand on that hip joint. Now turn your toes in, then out again. You will distinctly feel the movement in your hip joint. The correction must be made from the hip joint, but don't ask a rider to do it if it causes any pain in their hip.

When the rider is sitting in the saddle ask them to lift, say, their left seat bone and put it down again in the saddle as far away from their right seat bone as possible. Now ask them to lift their right seat bone and put it down in the saddle as far away from their left seat bone as possible. This action alters the angle of the ball joint within the socket and brings the rider's feet into a line more parallel with the horse's sides.

This exercise also gets a rider to sit down deeper into the saddle and helps a rider who sits tight in the saddle with both cheeks of their bottom firmly clenched together so that they look and feel perched on top of the horse.

Toes in when standing

Again, this depends on the angle at which the ball is set in the socket of the hip joint. The act of sitting in the saddle with their legs and knees further apart than when standing alters the angle of the ball and socket joint of the hip so the feet are now more likely to be parallel to the horse's sides anyway.

One leg longer than the other

Many people are born with one leg slightly longer than the other. When they are standing straight and upright they will feel that they are taking more weight on their longer leg and may also feel that the heel of the shorter leg is hardly touching the ground. Or they may feel that when one leg is straight, the knee of the other, longer, leg is slightly bent. If, when you adjust their stirrups, they feel that the stirrup leather on the short side is too long they may be able to sit straight and in balance more easily if that side is always one hole shorter. Check from the back as they ride round to see if they do sit straighter and with their weight equal on both seat bones after their stirrups have been readjusted and are no longer the same length.

Weak ankles

Many people have weak ankles and the ankles of older riders can become weaker and cause pain. Injuries to an ankle can leave a weakness there. Some people may feel that their ankle is collapsing outwards and their weight is falling out onto their little toe.

Weak ankles can be a very painful condition and a rider who suffers from it may be made to feel insecure in that it affects the whole leg which often feels weak as well.

I know about this because I developed the condition quite suddenly. I put support bandages in a figure-of-eight round my foot and ankle but it didn't help much and made my boots tight. I noticed that it felt much worse if, when my foot was in the stirrup, the stirrup leather had slipped across to the inside of the stirrup iron thus making the bearing surface of the stirrup slope outwards and downwards towards my little toe.

To alleviate the condition, I got a small piece of thick leather, punched two holes in it, put it through the inside of the slot in the stirrup iron and stitched it firmly in place. Thus, the stirrup leather was always kept to the

A small piece of thick leather (arrowed) sewn in to keep the stirrup leather on the outside of the iron. This arrangement supports the rider's ankle by raising the outside of the stirrup iron, thereby alleviating pain in the ankle itself.

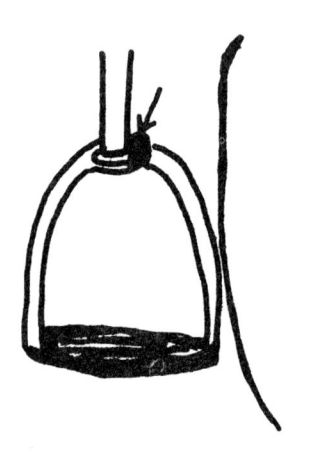

outside of the slot and the bearing surface of the stirrup iron was always tilted down towards my big toe and slightly raised on the outside near my little toe. I experienced no more pain and could ride all day with this new arrangement.

Narrow leathers in a wide slot in the stirrup iron can cause the same problem and can likewise be corrected with a piece of leather.

Another, but more expensive, possibility – and one that gives even more lift to the outside of the stirrup iron – is to buy sloping stirrup treads which are built up on one side, and to use them with the high side on the outside.

Several of my pupils over the years have complained of aching ankles but I never gave it much thought until it happened to me!

5 Bits and reins

For novice riders teach lessons on school horses wearing the mildest bit possible. Different riders, unbalanced and with unsteady hands are much better suffered with a mild bit in the horse's mouth; for the horse, jumping with beginners is less of an ordeal if the occasional jab in the mouth is from a mild bit. Your instructions should, of course, prevent this happening.

Lessons on pupils' own horses

Check if the bit fits the horse and if it is at the correct height in the horse's mouth. See if the horse is happy in the bit or fussing, opening its mouth, crossing its jaw and constantly trying to evade the bit. Is it the bit, the horse's teeth (perhaps sharp) or the rider's hands?

Horses can be uptight, jogging, reluctant to go forward with a too severe bit in their mouths. Riders may tell you that they have got a curb bit on because they can't stop the horse in anything else. Going round and round in an indoor school or a fenced small outdoor area that horse is soon going to realise that there is nowhere to go, so you can safely remove the curb chain and see what happens. (Don't risk doing this in an open field.) Very often the horse will relax and so will the rider. Encourage the rider to school the horse and to have lessons in a milder bit.

A jointed ring bit that is too wide for the horse will hang down low in a "V" in the centre of the mouth and it will be very easy for a horse to get its tongue over it. A bit that is too wide for the horse can slide across from one side of its mouth to the other and the joint will then often come onto the bars of the mouth when the rider turns the horse. Many 16hh Thoroughbred horses have very narrow bottom jaws and only need the same width of bit as a 12.2hh pony. It is not the height of the animal but the width of its lower jaw which tells you the size of bit it needs.

Bits and reins **45**

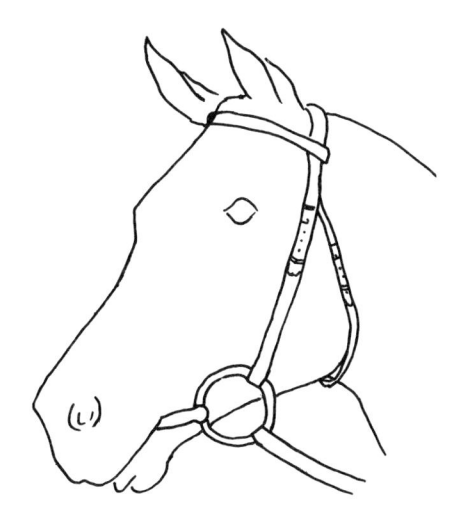

A bit which is too wide for the horse will hang low in its mouth. This makes it easy for the horse to get its tongue over the bit.

A jointed ring snaffle hangs at a different height and a different angle to a jointed snaffle with cheeks held in place by "keepers". The latter sits much higher in the mouth so the horse will find it more difficult to get its tongue over the bit. Pressure comes on different parts of the horse's mouth.

It is easier to guide a horse and keep it straight, for instance, when riding show jumping or cross-country, in a bit with cheeks. Horses seem less inclined to lean on a bit set a little higher in their mouths.

Snaffle bits (reading from left, 1–5): 1=too wide, hangs too low in the mouth and easy to get tongue over; 2=turning joint is on bars of the mouth; 3=correct fit; 4=cheek snaffle with keepers sits higher in the mouth; 5=cheek snaffle too wide and the joint sticks up into the roof of the mouth causing pain.

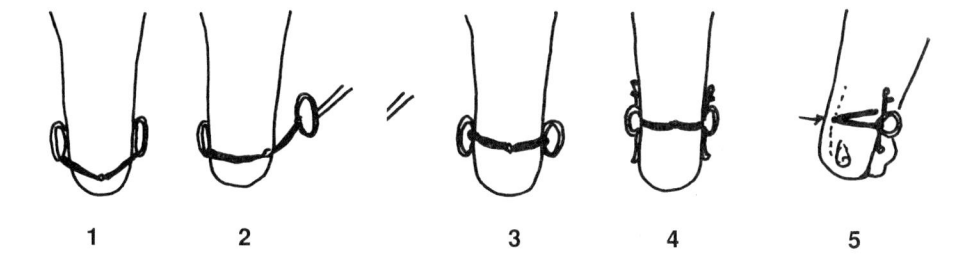

46   Teaching Riding

Single jointed snaffle bit with wire rings.

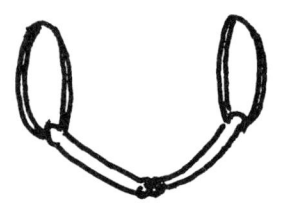

Single joint cheek snaffle. If this is worn without keepers attached to the bridle cheeks it will hang as low in the horse's mouth as a ring snaffle.

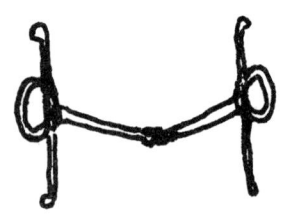

Cheek snaffle with keepers and French link joint.

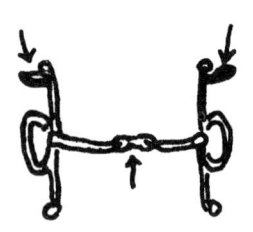

Keepers hold the cheeks upright so that the bit is held up higher in the horse's mouth.

Many horses go particularly well in a French snaffle. This has two joints and a small figure-of-eight centrepiece. There is less "nutcracker" action round the bottom jaw than with a single joint snaffle. A French link is allowed in dressage tests. It is made with and without cheeks.

Bitless bridles – reins on noseband

When a horse used for teaching seems unhappy in its mouth it may go better in a mild bitless bridle. Simply moving the reins from the bit onto the noseband or onto the side rings of a drop noseband can sometimes work wonders. (Only do this in a small fenced area the first time you try it.)

Those horses that are frightened of their mouths when jumping may go very differently like this. But only use this method in open fields if you have tried it out in a smaller area first and you are sure the rider has sufficient control of the horse.

Length of reins

I think that thick rubber reins tend to make the rider grasp them firmly and that with these reins they may develop insensitive hands. Another disadvantage is that it is difficult to let them slip through your hands if you want to give a horse more rein when jumping. These reins do have a place, however, on a horse which is very strong and difficult to hold and they are also helpful on a wet day as they will not slip through your hands so easily.

I would rather teach riders using a plain leather rein – not too thick or wide – as I find they then have more sensitive and sympathetic hands and are less inclined to "steer" using their hands far more than their legs to guide and control the horse.

Reins too short

If a rider holds the reins much too short with their hands halfway along the horse's neck they are going to pull themselves forward onto their front two seat bones and will feel that they are tipping forward, unbalanced and very insecure. Beginners and nervous riders often constantly over-shorten their reins and hold the horse tightly in the hope that it will not go faster.

Reins too short. The rider is pulled forward onto their fork. In this position the rider's lower leg is too far back.

Sitting in this position and holding the reins tightly will quickly upset a responsive horse and may make the horse stop and then go backwards because the pressure is still on the reins and therefore on its mouth. The rider often then pulls even harder on the reins because, "They are the brakes aren't they?" The horse then runs back into a fence or ditch or even falls over or rears up.

One of the very earliest lessons must be on what to do if a horse stops then goes backwards. For safety, the lesson should be given on how to ride forward into halt and push the hands forward to ease any pressure on the mouth as soon as the horse halts obediently. Teach riders that if the horse steps back unasked they must ease pressure on its mouth by pushing their hands forward towards the bit and using their legs strongly.

Reins too long

There are two ways of riding with the reins too long:
1. Having the reins drooping in loops so that there is no contact on the horse's mouth and it wanders about wondering where the rider wants it to go next. (Many people have the false idea that having no contact is having good hands.) Passive, ineffective riders often wander about with their reins in loops. This must not be confused with deliberately riding on a loose rein in a straight line, when the rider uses legs, seat

Reins too long. There is tension in this rider's shoulders, elbows, wrists and hands. He is sitting out of balance, behind the movement.

and back to ride the horse forward and keep it straight. This is often included in dressage tests.
2. Riding effectively with seat, legs and back and having a contact on the horse's mouth but with such a long rein that the upper arm is at an angle behind the body and the elbows are sticking out behind the rider's back or sideways. All these peculiar angles of arms and elbows are used in an effort to maintain a controlling contact on the horse's mouth with such very long reins. The rider has to sit back behind their hands and behind the movement, leaning back way out of balance with the horse in an attempt to maintain contact with its mouth. Some quite experienced riders get into this position and do not realise the cause of their problem in guiding and controlling their horse.

A helpful suggestion is to tell your pupils to, "Shorten your reins, keep them in a straight line and have a contact on the horse's mouth so it knows where both your hands are and you know where both corners of its mouth are." Another suggestion you can also try is, "If the telephone wires are down you can't get the message through. Keep the wires up and straight and the horse will get the message."

Perhaps the most effective suggestion of all is to pretend to loosen the bit in the cheek pieces of the bridle and tell the rider that if they don't keep a contact on their reins and hold the bit gently up into the horse's mouth it will fall out of its mouth and end up round its chest. When done convincingly this ruse has produced some very good results!

Learning to hold the reins at the correct length

How can you help riders to learn at what length to hold their reins? A very effective way is to firmly wind coloured elastic bands round the reins at a comfortable length for horse and rider when at walk – at which gait the bands will be out of sight inside the rider's hands. To trot they will shorten the reins and their hands will be just beyond the bands a little nearer to the horse's mouth. This adjustment is necessary because the horse carries its head higher in trot and therefore there is a shorter distance from the horse's mouth to the rider's hand.

Let pupils get the feel of riding with their reins at the correct length and then, when they are confident that they can do it unaided, remove the elastic bands.

Many beginners shorten the inside rein as they turn a corner then when they are on the straight of the school again their inside rein remains shorter, the horse's head is pulled inwards and it probably turns into the centre. Combine using elastic bands on the reins with the explanation that, "As a horse turns the inside of its neck is shortened but the outside of its neck is lengthened but after the turn both sides become the same length again so there is no need to shorten your inside rein. Just bring your hand back a little towards your body, ask for the turn and push your outside hand forward a little towards the horse's mouth to allow the turn." Obviously, you include using the legs to turn and ride forward but that simple basic explanation of how to use the reins is easy to understand and carry out. Once the rider has got the correct feel and movement remove the elastic bands.

You are there to help the rider to gain confidence and improve quickly. Don't be frightened to try things out, but try them out yourself first then you may realise what a help such ideas can be.

Small children holding the reins

Be aware of the very real danger of the loop of long reins hanging down below a small child's foot in such a position that the loop of rein could become caught up round their foot. If the pony suddenly dived its head down the loop could jerk the child off.

If the child fell off the loop of rein wrapped round the child's ankle could hold its foot in the stirrup and it could be dragged along by a terrified pony. This has happened, so be very aware of the danger and always be ready to shorten dangerous loops by putting a knot in them to keep them well above the child's foot. (This potentially dangerous situation can also occur when riders shorten their stirrups to jump. Loops which were safe before now hang down below the rider's foot. Check for this when giving a jumping lesson.)

Some people knot a child's reins together so that they are always at the same length. The advantage of this is that the child cannot drop one rein, which they often do, and so lose control. The disadvantages are:
1. The reins are the same length whatever gait the pony is in even though the height of its head, therefore the distance from its mouth to the child's hand, will vary.
2. The child will find it difficult to use only one hand and rein at a time.
3. The child will hold the reins with flat hands, knuckles upwards, palms down. This will become a habit that may be difficult to cure as they will become stiff in their shoulder, elbow, wrist and hand. Their elbows will tend to stick out.

Elastic bands do help but they may tend to slip through tiny hands. A thin narrow rein with a very small knot which can fit inside the hand at a length comfortable for pony and rider at walk seems to work well. Children soon learn to move their hand up the rein in front of the knot towards the pony's mouth when they want to trot or have more accurate control. They can use their reins correctly, thumbs on top, fingernails looking towards each other, from the beginning.

Grass reins

Horses and particularly little ponies can dive their heads down to eat grass and perhaps pull their riders over their heads or just wrench their

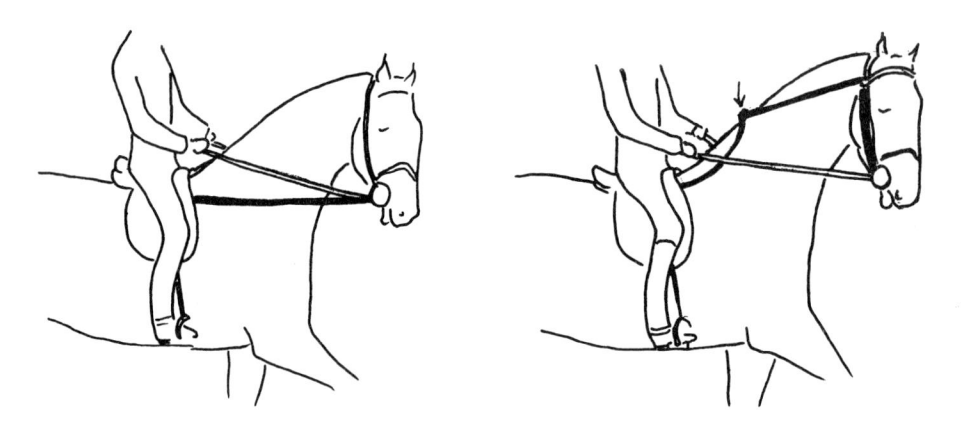

Grass reins. They need to be very restricting (left) *and quite tight to stop a determined pony eating grass. In this position they must be removed before the pony is jumped. Grass reins* (right) *can be adjusted to allow forward but not downward stretching. In this position they can be used for jumping the horse. The knot on the crest* (arrowed) *is essential to prevent the grass being reached.*

arms. Grass reins can easily be made from two pieces of cord or even two pieces of baling twine. If the animals are not going to be asked to jump, grass reins can be attached to the bit at each side, knotted on the top of the poll then attached to the "Ds" on each side of the front of the saddle. If there are no "Ds" they can be attached to the stirrup bars but not so that they prevent the stirrup leathers sliding off. They should be adjusted tight enough to prevent the animal from grazing but loose enough not to interfere with its natural head carriage. They can also be fitted to the second girth strap on each side (putting them on the first one can pull the saddle forward).

Grass reins to be used for jumping should go from each side of the bit up the line of the cheek pieces and be threaded through the loops of the brow band before being knotted on the crest and attached to the saddle in the same way. This method gives the animal the freedom to stretch its neck out to jump but still prevents it reaching down to eat grass.

If permanently used on the same animal the grass reins can be left on the bridle and have clips attached at the correct length which will fit on the saddle "Ds" for speed when putting on and taking off the saddlery.

Other uses

Grass reins which go from the bit to a knot on the crest then to the saddle "Ds" help to control small ponies which are inclined to misbehave. Psychologically, the slight contact on their mouths makes them feel that they are being controlled. They are less likely to try to get their heads down and buck. When a child tries to turn using one rein only (as many do) the pony cannot end up with its head turned right round onto the child's knee but still going in the direction in which it wants to go. The rein on the outside prevents the pony's neck turning in a U-bend.

A strong, fresh horse on the lunge, perhaps for exercise, can be easier to control and more respectful of you if it is wearing grass reins. They will also prevent a horse being lunged in a grass field from constantly trying to eat.

6   Whips and hands

Any child or adult who carries a whip should be taught to put their whip in their left hand with their reins when they mount – always, every time.

If they only remember to do this on special occasions instead of making it a regular habit they may one day have an accident with a young or nervous horse. The horse will see the whip waving about in the rider's right hand as they are mounting and because it sees the whip with its right eye it may shy towards the rider, away from the whip, and knock them over.

The angle at which the whip lies is a great giveaway of the rider's hand position and the tension in their whip hand. If there is a decent-sized knob on the top of a whip there is no need to hold the whip firmly (so putting extra tension in that hand) to stop it slipping down. If a whip has not got a knob a rubber martingale stop as used on the reins or the more rounded rubber stop used where the martingale and neckstrap meet on the horse's chest make excellent substitutes.

A knob or stop can rest between the middle joint of the rider's thumb and their index finger. There is no need to grasp the whip or put any extra tension on the whip hand to keep the whip in place.

The correct position of a whip

The correct position in which to hold a whip is listed below. The list shows you what an interesting and varied number of faulty hand positions (and therefore stiffness in the whip hand) you can discover if you look carefully at each rider's whip!

1. If the hands are held still in the normal riding position, thumbs on top, fingernails towards each other, the end of the whip will lie across the centre of the rider's thigh.
2. If the rider's thumb goes up the whip and presses against it the result is to produce in the rider's hand (and therefore also in the elbow and

Whips and hands 55

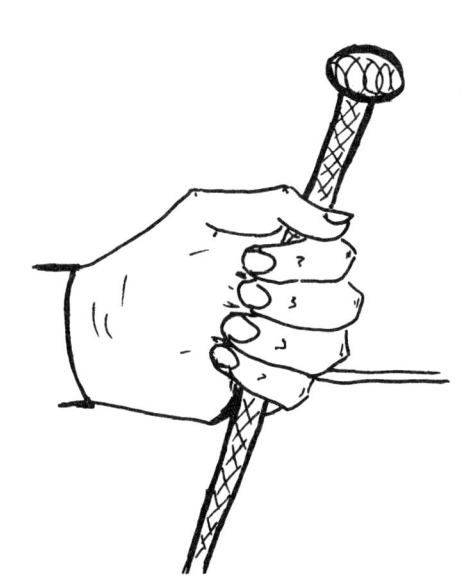

Hand positions for holding a whip. The whip (left) *is held incorrectly; it has to be held too firmly to keep it in this position. Tension in the whip hand can be felt by the horse through the rein contact.*

The whip (below) *is held correctly. The knob is resting lightly between the index finger and the thumb and there is no tension in the hand.*

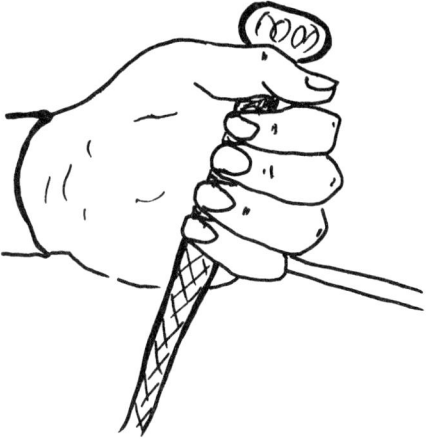

The whip (left) *is held incorrectly; there is tension in the hand holding the whip up and tension in the thumb pressing against the whip. Again, the horse will feel the tension in the rider's whip hand.*

56 Teaching Riding

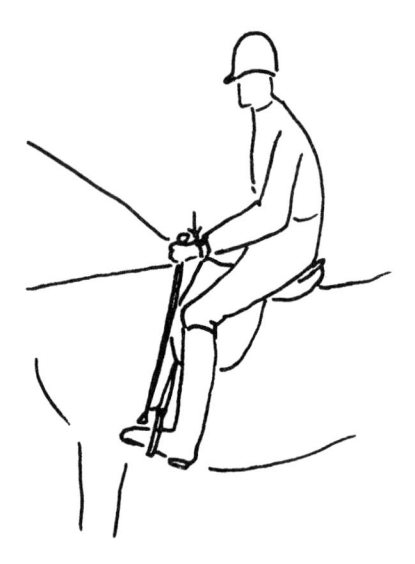

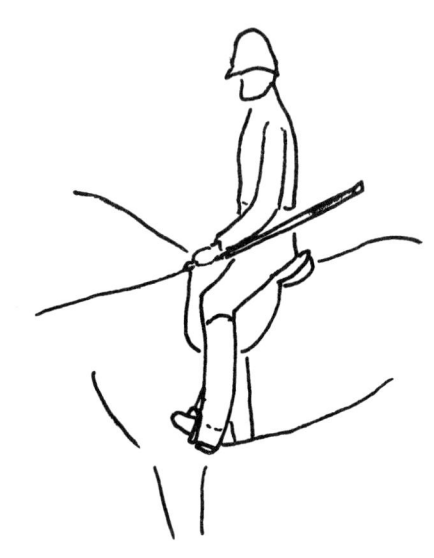

Incorrect position (above). The wrist (arrowed) of the whip hand is too hollow; the hand is stiff and the rider's back has collapsed.

Incorrect position (above, right). The too stiff whip hand has caused stiffness in the wrist, elbow and shoulder. The rider's leg, too, is too stiff and is bracing against the stirrup.

Correct position (right). The whip is held correctly in the rider's hand, knob resting against the thumb, whip lying midway across the rider's thigh. The rider's whip hand and leg are in a soft natural position.

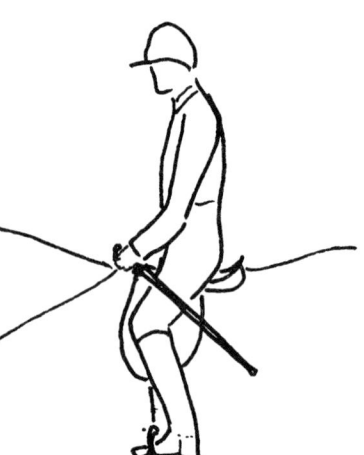

shoulder) a stiffness which the horse can feel in its mouth on that side. To avoid this stiffness, the rider's thumb should be gently round the whip not up it.

3. If the thumb of the whip hand is pointing stiffly down towards the horse's mouth the wrist will also stiffen and the end of the whip will follow the line of the rider's forearm.

Whips and hands   57

4. If the hands are held flat, knuckles on top, the end of the whip will stick straight out to the side. The rider's joints will stiffen.
5. If the wrist is hollowed downwards, thumb still on top, but now much higher than the wrist, the end of the whip will lie vertical, down the horse's shoulder in front of the rider's knee.
6. If the whip is held turned over a little, thumb towards the horse's head, fingernails uppermost, the end of the whip will lie inside the rider's forearm, close to their body and the tip will appear near the elbow.

Changing the whip hand

When holding a short whip take both reins into the same hand as the whip and with the free hand take hold of the whip as usual with the thumb near to the knob.

Draw the whip gently up out of the rein hand, put it in the normal position and then pick up the other rein. If the whip is changed when one rein is still in each hand it is an ugly and clumsy procedure involving lifting the whip and one rein high over the withers to the other side. Movement of the bit in the horse's mouth and probably jerking of the reins will occur.

To change a long whip there must be a different plan because this whip is too long to draw up through the rein hand. Put both reins into the whip hand. Turn the free hand so that the thumb is towards the whip's knob and the little finger towards its tip. The elbow of this hand will be point-

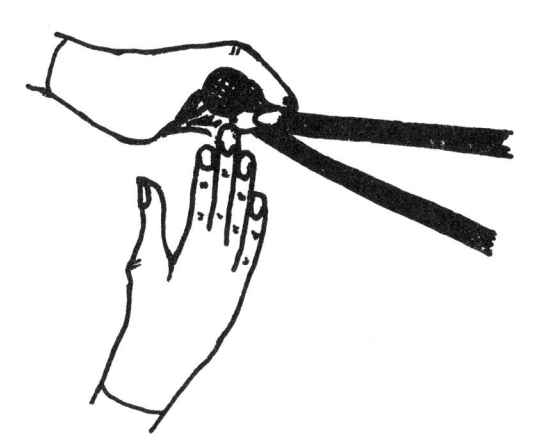

Changing the short whip correctly from left to right hand.

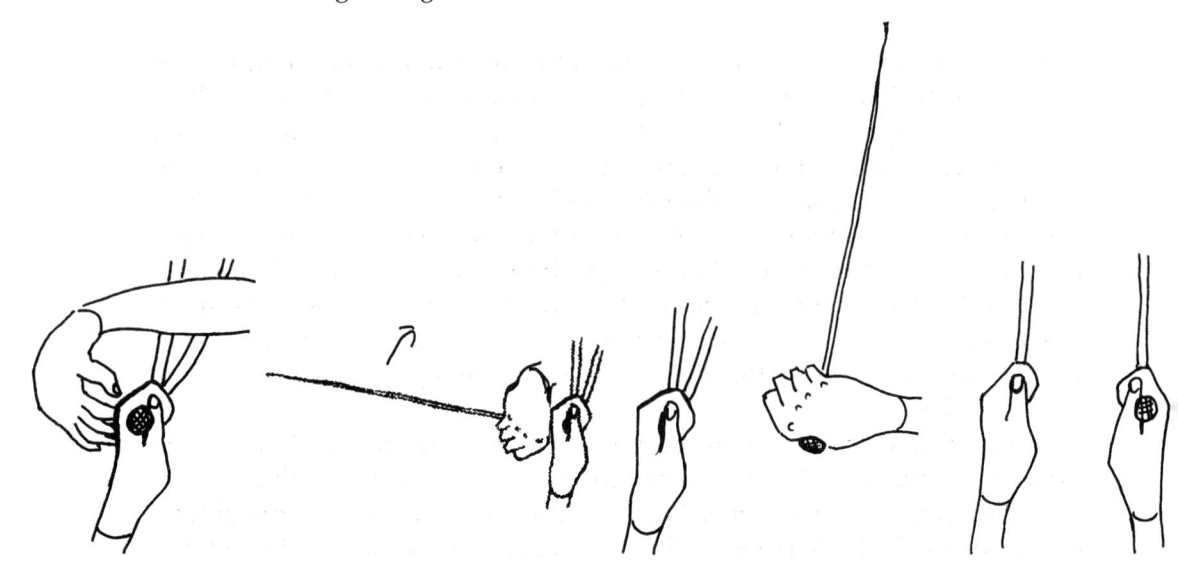

Changing to a long whip up over the withers.

ing towards the horse's head, so it is quite a big movement of this arm. Take hold of the whip below the hand now holding the whip and reins. Release the whip from the rein hand and slowly turn it so that its tip passes up and over the withers pointing towards the sky until it comes into position again across the rider's other thigh. Some horses are frightened when seeing a long whip being changed high above their withers so warn riders first.

Some horses are frightened of long whips being carried at all. Some horses get into a dangerous panic if any whip is carried by their rider. If a horse panics tell the rider to drop their whip. Some riders freeze in panic themselves in this situation and just hang on to everything including the whip. You may have to go on and on saying, "Drop the whip, drop the whip," until you eventually get through to them. Having probably been whizzing round away from the whip the horse is likely to stand stock still, shaking, as soon as the whip is dropped.

Perhaps something terrifying connected with a whip has happened in that horse's life. If so, it is unlikely to ever forget.

Small children may find a whip and reins difficult to manage but something looking like a whip works likes a "magic wand" with many little ponies. Having been "dead idle" and refusing to trot or canter for their small rider they brighten up and become responsive. I have achieved great success by presenting the rider with a piece of straw no more than 30cm (12in) long. I make quite sure that the pony sees that I am carrying this "whip" and that its rider has now got it in their hand. Just ask the rider to move the hand with the rein and straw in it. The pony sees the straw move and thinks that the rider has now got a whip. That "magic wand" works very well without the inconvenience of having to try to hold a whip in a small hand.

A thin twig with a piece of rag tied round it to form a knob at the top (or thick elastic) can also be an easy to carry substitute for a whip.

Unless you want the horse to know that you are passing the rider a whip, approach the horse with the whip behind your back and hand it to the rider when you are really close to them. Some horses are frightened when a person on foot holds a whip out towards them.

Using a whip

Short whips should only be used behind the rider's leg when both reins have been put into the other hand. If a short whip is used behind the rider's leg when the whip hand is still holding the rein the horse's mouth will be quite severely jerked. A horse can, however, be woken up or "reminded" of the whip by a quick tap on the shoulder when there is still a rein in the whip hand because that movement only involves a quick turn of the wrist. This is a useful thing to teach small children who tend to get in a muddle with their reins if expected to put both reins in one hand every time they use their whip but it is not the correct way to use a whip to get a horse to go forward.

If a horse is bulging its shoulder out to lead the way that it wants to go and turning its head in the opposite direction, hanging towards home for instance, the whip can be used sharply several times on the leading shoulder. The rider's outside rein on that side should try to get the horse to bend its head and neck the other way and the leg on the outside should try to control the sideways movement.

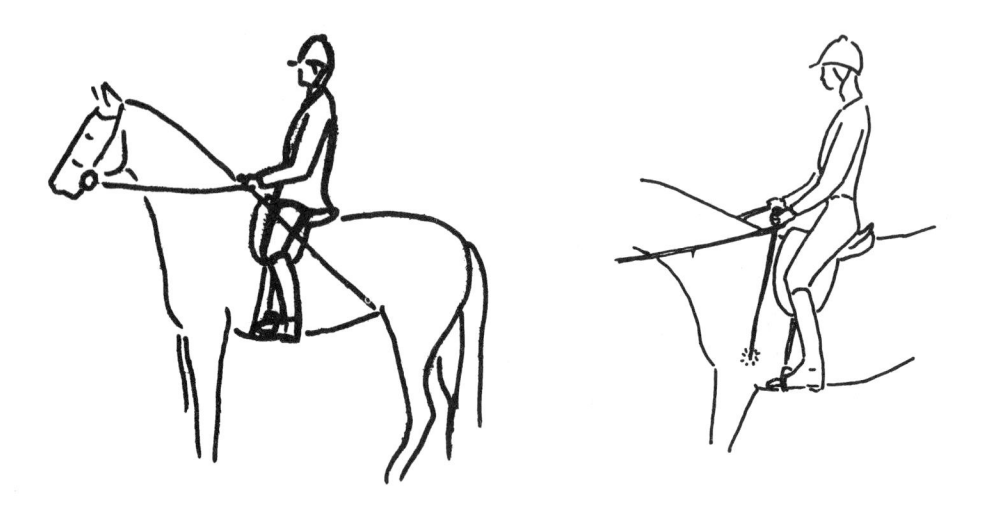

Correct position in the saddle (left). *The rider sits in balance on the horse and is using the whip correctly. If his horse was whisked from under him this rider would land in balance on his feet. The correct way* (right) *of using the whip to prevent the horse's shoulder bulging.*

A long whip can also be used on the shoulder when a horse is falling in on circles. The rider must prevent this happening by tap, tap, tapping on the horse's inside shoulder before that shoulder starts to bulge inwards. To be effective that whip hand must be carried out a little way from the horse's neck so that the tip of the whip can tap the horse just in front of its elbow as lightly or as strongly as is necessary.

The whip hand is also the hand holding the rein that is asking for the inside bend on the circle so action of whip and rein must be well coordinated. The rider's inside leg must also be used to keep the horse out on the circle and to keep it going forward.

Using a whip to make the horse go forward

In this case the whip must be used behind the rider's leg. While it may be effective to use a long whip with the reins still held one in each hand it is essential to put both reins in one hand to be effective with a short whip.

One really hard smack usually works better than several half-hearted taps with a horse which is for some reason reluctant to go forward.

If the horse is genuinely frightened of something do not tell its rider to

Whips and hands 61

The correct way to ride a horse forward using a long whip

hit the horse. If you were really frightened of something and someone tried to make you go up to it wouldn't you fight even more against going nearer? So will the horse. Give it a second or two to look and think. The rider should indicate with reins and legs a track not quite so close to whatever it is the horse is frightened of. After a few seconds of thought the horse may decide that it is not so terrifying after all, relax and walk on taking a curving track not quite so near the "horror".

Tell your pupils, "If you hit a genuinely frightened horse for not passing, for instance, a flapping plastic sheet, you are likely to teach it to fight you by whipping round, rearing, trying to buck you off," and so on. Once learnt, the horse will use this behaviour again to get its own way.

Many people always carry their whips and use them only in their right hand. This is one reason why carrying and using your whip in your left hand can have a startling effect on a lot of horses!

The whip is not intended to save the rider using his or her legs but to reinforce them. Ask a horse to go forward from a squeeze of the legs and if it does not immediately do so, use the whip sharply behind the leg. Teach the horse that if it answers to a squeeze it will not be hit. If it is slow to respond it will. If a horse is always kicked rather than squeezed as the first aid to walk forward it will always need to be kicked. A squeeze, then if necessary a sharp tap with a whip, can teach a horse to answer to a lighter aid. Practise this with your ride. Even lazy animals can be improved.

Hands

Unfortunately, there is a tendency for instructors to tell riders to keep their hands down low without considering the height at which the horse is carrying its head, the length of arm from shoulder to elbow of the rider or the straight line of elbow, wrist, hand, rein, bit.

If a horse has a naturally high head carriage or if it is carrying its head unnaturally high the rider cannot bring the horse's head down by lowering their hands, nor hold it down by setting their hands low.

The position of the rider's hand. Hands held too low (right); too high (below, right); and (below) at the correct level and in the correct position.

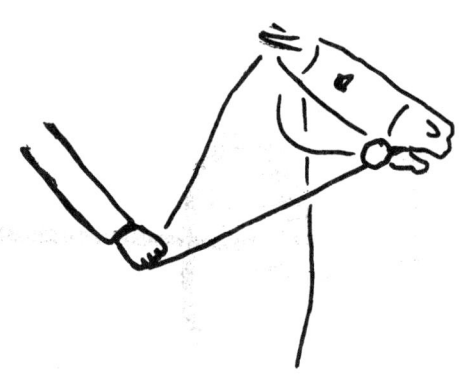

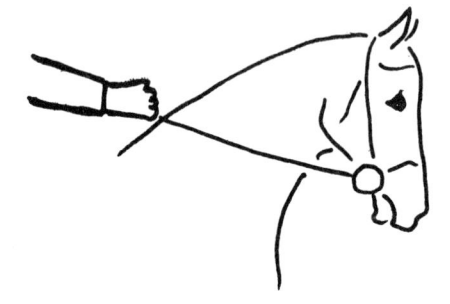

As soon as the rider's hand becomes the lowest point in the line from elbow to bit there will be tension in the rider's shoulders, elbow, wrist and hand. This stiffness can be felt in the horse's mouth so it often resists the feel of the bit by perhaps raising its head more, opening its mouth or crossing its jaw and setting itself against this set pressure.

The position of the rider's hand effects the kind of tension on the rein which the horse feels through the bit. If the hands are held knuckles upmost, thumbs facing each other there is an unnatural twist in the rider's forearm and this creates tension in their hands, wrists, elbows and shoulders. If their thumbs are upmost, fingernails facing each other there is no tension (unless the rider is gripping the reins very tightly). Try this yourself when sitting in a chair.

The position of the rider's hand. Correct (left), *a soft, sympathetic hand with the thumb on top and the fingernails facing each other and in sight of the rider. To help a rider* (below, left) *to soften their hands, let the rein come from the horse's mouth into the rider's hand as here, via the thumb and index finger and leave the hand between the third and little finger.*

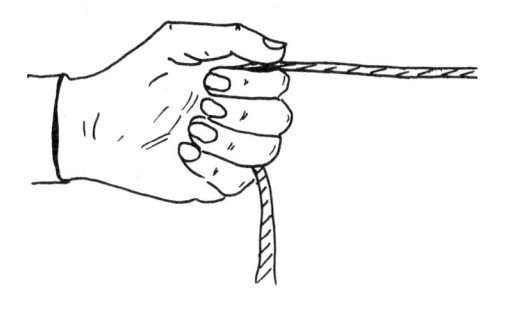

First, pretend to hold the reins knuckles upmost, thumbs facing each other and move your arms forwards and backwards as if you are following the movement of the horse's head at walk. Now do the same thing with thumbs up, fingernails facing or almost in an "Are your nails clean?" position. You will notice that your shoulder and arm joints move much more freely in the second position. Let your pupils try this experiment too. Ask them if their nails are clean and they will naturally turn their hands into the softer position.

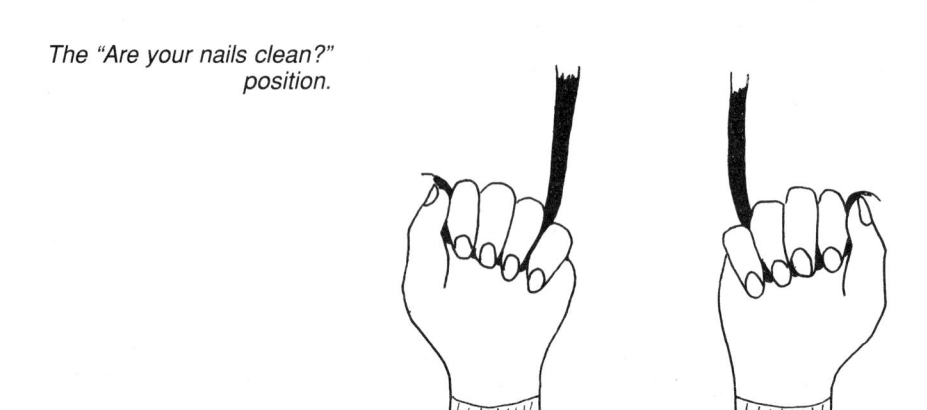

The "Are your nails clean?" position.

If anyone has really stiff, low set hands tell them to completely alter the way in which they are holding their reins. Let the reins come from the horse's mouth into their hand between their thumb and their index finger and leave their hands between the third and little finger. Holding the reins in this way gives riders a really soft feel and is the quickest way I know of improving heavy or hard hands.

An interesting side effect is that many horses will now go quite differently, happier in their mouths and more relaxed.

After using this method with people on their own horses I have found that several have been amazed by the difference in their horses and said that they have never before gone so well. Try it yourself. I think you and your ride will be surprised and pleased by the results.

Whips and hands 65

Pupils with a hand problem should continue to hold their reins in this way for several lessons before changing back to normal. If the habit reccurs revert to the "soft" rein holding method.

Having two reins on a snaffle bit and holding them as if they were the reins of a double bridle can also soften a rider's hands.

Circles and turns

Many riders drop their inside hand lower when riding a circle at any gait. Notice this and correct it. Lowering the inside hand actually says to the horse, "Don't step under with your inside leg." When used low the inside rein affects the inside hind leg and makes it more difficult for the horse to step forward and under with that leg as it has to do on a circle if working correctly from behind. The low inside hand also affects the inside foreleg by shortening its stride.

Go down on your hands and knees and bring your head round and down as if on a small circle so that you can feel what an effort it is to take

Faults: the inside hand (left) *dropping as the rider rides on a circle to the left; and* (right) *the rider is pushing down with his hands which causes his shoulders to come forward.*

a step with your inside leg (simulating the horse's hind leg) and notice that your arm (simulating the horse's foreleg) also feels restricted. Now do exactly the same thing with your head up in a natural position. You will be amazed by the extra freedom to use your inside limbs. The same is true in turns and during serpentines so watch your riders very carefully – most drop one hand more than the other. Some only drop one hand and always the same one. Correct the riders by constantly saying, "Lift your inside hand." Use an overcorrection and get them to always have their inside hand higher than their outside hand. They will then begin to think for themselves, hopefully notice a different feel in their hand and the fact that their horse is now freer and easier on turns and circles and is stepping under more than before.

Transitions

Changing from one gait to another needs thought and preparation. When a horse changes gait it needs to alter its balance, and therefore its centre of gravity, and prepare its muscles, so the rider must warn the horse that something different is going to happen. The rider should use half-halts, which is just another name for preparing and re-balancing the horse. They must ride their horse forward with their legs into a slightly holding, but not pulling back, hand. The horse will step under its body a little more with its hind legs and so move its centre of gravity further back, lighten its forehand and be ready to respond to the rider's aids.

Transitions up

To go forward from walk to trot the rider's body weight moves slightly forward as they ride the horse forward with their legs and seat into their hands which keep a light contact on the horse's mouth but allow it to go forward into trot. The rider must continue to ride forward as gently or strongly as is necessary for their horse to keep an even rhythm of trot. If the horse is a bit lazy the rider should feel the rhythm of trot as it just begins to slow down and ride forward more strongly, not wait until the horse drops to walk leaving them frantically trying to get it trotting again.

A smooth transition to canter comes from the last few strides of trot being a little lighter and more active but in the same rhythm. A horse needs to be lighter in front to make an easy upward transition to canter.

Many horses and particularly little ponies go into a faster and faster and longer and longer trot before falling into an unbalanced canter. No half-halts have been learnt or used. The rider's loose reins and frantically kicking legs are saying, "Go on, trot faster," and that is just what the horse or pony is doing. The very simple suggestion, "Steady your horse," in trot so that your hands are saying "Don't trot fast," and your legs are saying "Come on, canter," can help such a horse and rider.

Transitions down

To slow down, a horse moves its centre of gravity further back towards its tail. Its hind legs take more weight and its forehand lightens. The rider's weight and therefore their centre of gravity should move back a little further as the rider uses half-halts to lighten the horse's forehand and make it step under more with its hind legs. The rider must ride the horse forward into a slightly holding hand and *think* "trot" and "trot on" so that the horse will not drop back into trot with a jolt. This happens when the horse is pulled back into trot with the reins only with no half-halts as preparation.

From trot down to walk the same things apply. Half-halt, weight slightly back, ride forward into a holding hand and *think* "walk" and "walk on". Ride forward into all transitions down – yes, even into halt.

To halt, sit tall, weight back a little, close your legs to ride forward and think "halt". Raise your hands a fraction and don't drop them or you will stop the horse stepping under with its hind legs and standing square. When the horse has halted push your hands forward a little to ease the feel on its mouth. (Leaning back and using the seat bones very strongly can make sensitive horses go hollow and come up above the bit.)

Very many riders drop their hands when going into transitions down and use their reins too strongly. They may all know that when going into transitions down the horse should step under more with its hind legs yet their action of lowering their hands actually prevents the horse stepping under or at least makes it very difficult for the horse to do so. They mostly do not know that they are doing it as their hands go down unconsciously from habit. Look at your ride carefully as they ride transitions down. I'll bet that 50 per cent or more are guilty of this fault!

To correct them tell them to ride forward more into a transition down, to think of their weight coming very slightly back and their steady closed legs causing the transition down. Ask them to lift their hands a little into the transition down and think of riding the horse forward into the bit. Ask them to imagine that they are holding the bit up slightly in the horse's mouth. Taken literally this is an over-correction but as they will usually carry it out it will probably prove to be about right.

I am sure that you will have noticed how many horses resist when going into transitions down, raising their heads and hollowing their backs. For 90 per cent of the time the rider's lowered and stiffened hand is the cause. Practise transitions to walk and halt by riding forward and lifting the hands, using as little rein as possible. The aim should be to now get transitions without any resistance from the horse. Don't ask for transitions down at a certain marker as this encourages too much use of the reins. Just ask the riders individually for transitions in their own time but with no resistance. Say, "Lift your hands into transitions down" until they have ceased to want to lower them.

Better results can often be achieved by riding transitions down turning inwards onto a circle because the horse, stepping under with its inside hind leg, naturally puts its own centre of gravity further back and so finds it easier to decrease pace.

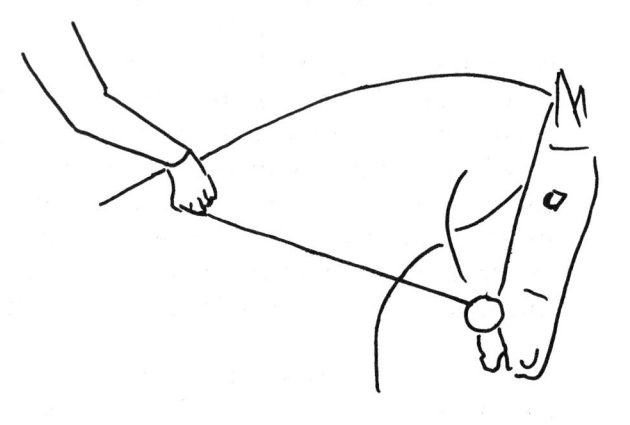

A common fault in transitions down. The rider's wrist is stiff, hollow and bent; the horse is likely to resist, raising its head and hollowing its back to reduce the effect on its mouth of this hand position or go overbent as here.

A very common fault in transitions down. The rider is bracing against the stirrups and his lower leg is coming forward.

A common fault is to stiffen the knee and brace against the stirrups. If the rider's lower leg comes forward you know this is their problem. To correct it say, "Relax your knee. Let your weight go onto your seat bones not onto your stirrups."

Transition to canter

Many horses, not necessarily lazy ones, will break into canter when asked but after a few strides will drop back into trot or have to be ridden forward very strongly to keep them cantering.

Very often the cause is the rider's low set hands. To canter in balance the horse must lower its hind quarters and step further under with its hind legs. When cantering on a circle the inside hind leg (one of the diagonal pair in the three-time of canter) must step well forward and under at every stride of canter so that the horse can easily maintain an effortless, balanced canter. Low set hands prevent the hind legs stepping forward and under sufficiently and make staying in canter difficult for the horse – so it reverts to trot.

Watch the horses which break from canter to trot after a few strides or which are very hard work to keep cantering and see if their riders' low set hand or hands could be the cause. To correct this ask them to lift their hands when asking for canter and keep them lifted as they ride forward to maintain canter. Explain that their hands had been preventing the horse cantering and now they must "allow" canter. Changing their way of holding the reins so that the reins will come in from the bit between their thumb and index finger and out by their little finger can prove an instant success with the horse and keep it cantering happily.

Because in order to canter a horse has to lower its quarters and round its back behind the saddle, reluctance to stay in canter can be caused by discomfort in the horse's back. Because it hurts when it canters the horse is reluctant to stay in canter – so it trots.

If changing the way of holding the reins makes no difference and the horse is still reluctant to stay in canter ask the rider to shorten their stirrups a couple of holes and sit forward out of the saddle, with their weight more into the inside stirrup as they ask for canter. Tell them to stay forward out of the saddle all the time. They must not set their hands down low, their hands must allow canter. This method works well with many horses which keep falling back into trot or are reluctant to canter. It is a clear sign that their backs are uncomfortable in canter with the rider's weight in the saddle. Without that weight on their backs it can be a very different picture. If discomfort in the back is now the suspected cause of the horse falling into trot, there are other signs you can look for (see Chapter 8).

Young horses learn to canter more easily and learn to round their backs and use them correctly if the rider's weight is out of the saddle when they first start canter work. The rider's weight can very gradually come into the saddle but they must never "sit heavy" on a young horse during its early work in canter. Strong use of the seat and back to keep a young horse cantering is inadvisable and can cause hollow back, resentment and even bucking. The hands must always allow canter.

In riding the rider's legs should be used 80 per cent or more and their hands only 20 per cent or less. Unfortunately it is usually the other way round. Often the rider's legs are used only 10 per cent as the horse is steered and hauled about by the reins and the reins are pulled strongly to slow it down or stop it.

7 Riding faults

Hands crossing over neck

When turning a horse many people allow both of their hands to move over to the direction in which they want to go. They often use the reins strongly as they do so, pulling on the wrong side of their horse's mouth as their hand crosses over the neck. The horse is confused and the rider gets cross not knowing what has caused the horse to be, as the rider thinks, disobedient. This is a very common fault and I have seen very many unhappy horses and riders in this situation.

Check your riders and make sure none of them are even slightly letting one hand "trespass" onto their other hand's side of the neck.

To correct this fault explain what is happening. Let them use their hands

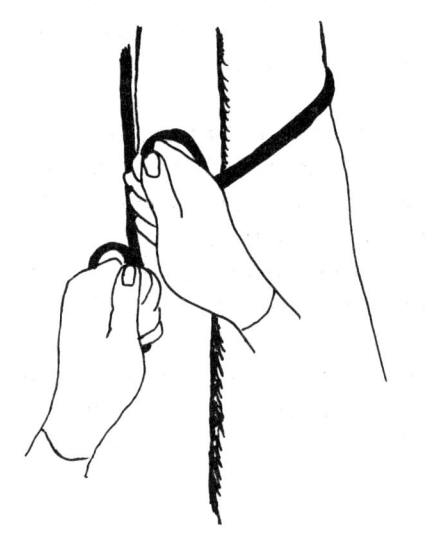

The rider's right hand crossing over the horse's neck.

as they were before and show them the pull coming on the wrong side of the horse's mouth. Now suggest that they consciously push their outside hand forward on its own side of the neck until they get out of the habit.

As they turn, the horse's neck shortens on the inside but it lengthens on the outside as the neck bends. The rider's outside hand must "allow" this lengthening.

Leg position

The rider's legs must hang naturally against the horse's side. The horse is round in its barrel and if the rider's lower legs are to be against the horse's sides the knee must be soft and loose.

If the knee is tight and close to the saddle the lower leg comes off the horse's sides.

If the rider has round thighs the thigh muscle must be pulled towards the back of the leg so that the area in contact with the saddle is as flat as possible. The feet should be parallel with the horse's sides if this can be achieved without stiffness.

The rider's legs should be used to give an inward squeeze with the inside of the lower leg. When not being used they should hang quietly against the horse's sides so that the warmth of the horse's tummy can be felt all of the time by the rider's lower leg. Because the horse is roughly barrel shaped if the knee is held tightly against the saddle the lower leg will come away from the horse's sides.

The knee must be relaxed and a little way away from the saddle for the lower leg to be on. Let your ride try this out. The heels should not be used. A horse should not be "kicked on". If it does not go forward to a squeeze of the lower legs it should be given a sharp tap with a whip behind the rider's leg. Hopefully, the horse will learn that if it goes forward to a squeeze it will not get hit and so it should become more responsive.

A horse that is always kicked as the first aid to go forward will always need to be kicked.

Toes down, heels frantically kicking, is a very common sight especially with children.

Toes out, back of the rider's calf against the horse's sides, is a common fault especially with riders who have short legs and round thighs. This position, gripping with the calf, is also a common fault that many riders make when jumping.

It is essential that riders learn to use each leg independently at a very early stage of learning to ride.

Bending in walk round barrels or cones is an ideal way to teach the use of alternate legs to beginners. The inside leg is used to keep the horse out a little away from the barrel as they go past it. The outside leg then takes over when they have passed the barrel and this leg nudges the horse across the gap between two barrels so that it will pass the next one on the opposite side.

Legs can be used both at once to squeeze or individually to nudge, nudge a horse away from the leg or to just press on a horse's side.

Legs and body weight should be used 80 per cent or more to guide and control a horse and hands only 20 per cent or less.

Unfortunately for the horse it is usually the other way round.

Use of spurs

Spurs should only be used by experienced riders. They should be used as a refined aid on a well schooled horse not to make an idle one go faster. Constant strong use of spurs and constant kicking deaden a horse's sides.

Spurs should be worn high up level with the seam of a riding boot. The buckle of the spur strap should be done up at centre front. If your spurs

Spurs: they are fitted (far left) *too low here. They should be worn high up level with the seam* (near left) *of a riding boot.*

have one long and one short arm the long arm should be worn on the outside. The neck of the spur should point downwards. Spurs with rowels should never be worn.

Legs

Some adult beginners think that you stay on a horse by grip – literally by clamping your legs round the horse like a vice.

For this reason explain to your ride, preferably before they even get on their horses, that they will learn to balance on their seat bones in the saddle and that their legs should hang down relaxed, following and touching the curve of the horse's sides as much as is possible.

The rider should be able to feel the warmth of the horse's sides coming through their jods or boots. Because of the curved shape of a horse's body

A soft knee allows the rider's lower legs to hang naturally. Each leg follows the curve of the horse's side.

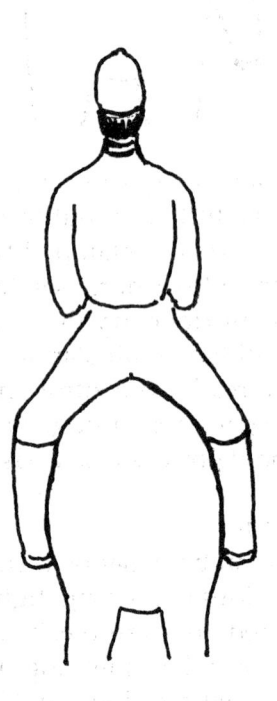

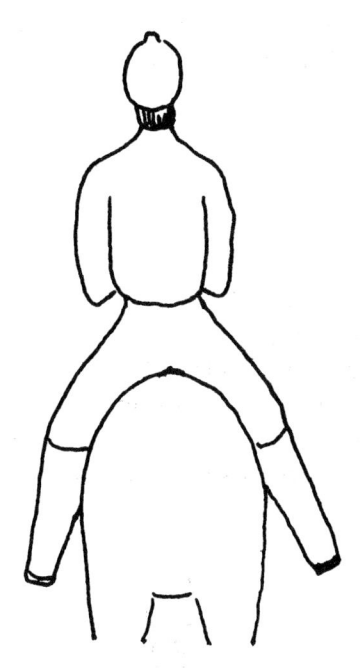

A tight, gripping knee. Riders who adopt this position stiffen their lower legs which are then not in contact with the horse's sides.

if their lower leg is in contact with their horse's sides their knee should be soft and a little way out from the saddle.

If their knee is clamped tightly on to the saddle their lower leg will be away from their horse's sides because of the curve of its body.

Let your riders try this out so that they can feel the difference for themselves. Riders of all standards can benefit from thinking about this; their legs are ready to control and guide the horse by using the inside of the lower leg to press, nudge or in extreme cases kick the horse's sides. In this position their legs also assist the rider with their balance.

Grip

Horses can be upset by a rider getting on and immediately clamping the horse's sides in a strong, tight grip. Grip is necessary if a horse is suddenly frightened; for example, by a dog jumping out. Grip can also assist a rider to stay on when jumping a fence or when a horse is misbehaving and trying to get the rider off. Grip is not used to keep the rider on the horse at walk, trot or canter. Balance keeps the rider relaxed and supple. Grip creates stiffness all over the rider – head, body, legs and hands.

Legs gripping up

Stirrup irons rattling and swinging about loosely below the rider's feet are a sign of gripping up. The rider has probably drawn their legs up a little as they clamped their calves on to their horse's sides because they think that this will help them to stay on. Sometimes the rider appears to be crouching their body.

This action of gripping up is often seen in sitting trot, in canter and if a horse shoots about or bucks. (Sometimes the cause is simply that the rider's stirrups are a bit too long.)

Suggest that they think, "Sit on your back two seat bones, sit tall, legs down long, heels nearer to the ground."

Length of stirrups

The length at which a person rides is absolutely crucial to their balance and stability in the saddle, their ability to have and maintain a correct position in the saddle and their effectiveness as a rider. One hole too long can be an absolute disaster whereas one hole too short will not do much harm.

So often I have seen instructors working their ride without stirrups to get them "deep" in the saddle without any instructions as to how to sit. Then when they take their stirrups back the instructor will say, "Who can

Three stirrup lengths: correct (far right); *stirrups too long and toe down* (centre); *and* (near right) *incorrect, heel forced down and ankle locked.*

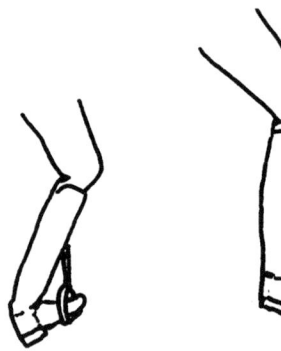

Riding faults 77

ride with longer stirrups now? Two holes down that is very good. Three holes longer that is wonderful." It isn't, it is often a major disaster because the pupil who might have been sitting upright and effective on their back two seat bones before has now got to reach down for their stirrups and to do so has rolled forward on their pelvis so that they are perched in the saddle, tipping insecurely forward onto their fork, onto their front two seat bones. They are insecure, unbalanced and ineffective yet have just been praised for ruining their riding!

"Sit on your bottom, sit on your two back seat bones and while keeping that 'feel' lift one leg off the saddle and lift it out then down and long. Now do the same with the other leg while at the same time sitting on your two back seat bones. You will ride deeper but without tipping forward."

A rider will have more control of a strong pulling horse or of one which

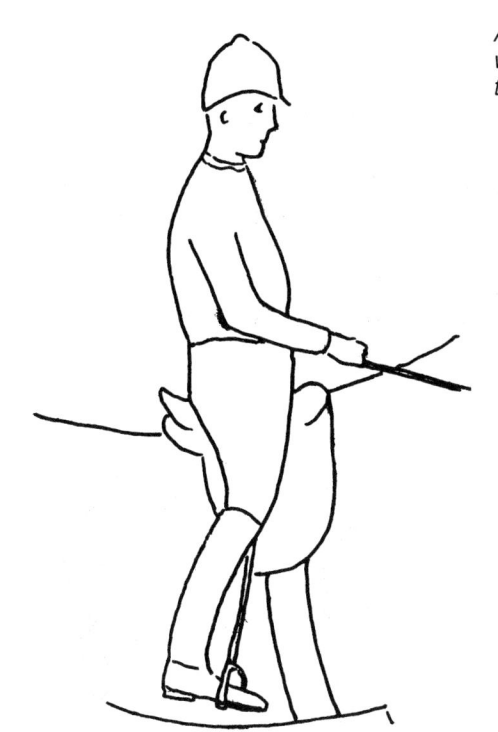

An insecure rider. He is sitting on his fork with his stirrups too long. His lower leg is too far back.

is misbehaving if they have their stirrup leathers one or two holes shorter than usual. When you have experimented and felt this yourself you can explain it to your ride with real understanding.

Teaching beginners to trot

From the start teach your beginners to sit on their bottoms – on their back two seat bones and to follow the movement of the horse's body at walk by allowing their stomachs and therefore also the small of their backs to move from upright to forward as the horse walks.

Far too many people collapse their backs as the horse walks and allow their stomachs and the small of their backs to sway backwards. Even beginners on the lead rein can put one hand in the small of their backs, palm outwards and learn to use and feel the correct forward movement of their backs at walk.

Sitting upright and feeling this forward movement of the small of the back at walk is the foundation for learning sitting trot and following this early preparation most riders should not find it a difficult thing to do.

I do not believe riders should be taught rising trot until they can ride a horse accurately and control it on turns, circles and serpentines, riding it forward with their back, seat and legs, sitting on their back two seat bones in sitting trot as they do so.

If they have this good foundation of position, balance and the use of their seat, back and legs they will pick up rising trot very quickly and will easily and naturally revert to sitting trot voluntarily when accurate riding is necessary or when a difference of opinion with the horse occurs.

Sitting trot

Sitting trot can be taught on the lead, on the lunge or in a class lesson according to the age and ability of pupils and the behaviour of the horses used. Adjust the stirrups to the correct length to enable the rider to sit on their back two seat bones and not tip on to their front two seat bones. Keep the rider's feet in their stirrups. They must allow their weight to drop onto their two back seat bones and must not stand in the stirrups, lean on their stirrups or push against their stirrups in any way. Pretend that the stirrup

Riding faults 79

A rider sitting deep and in balance in a good saddle which supports him.

leathers are very old, nearly broken and that if the rider leans on them at all they will break and the stirrup will drop off onto the ground. This image helps to ensure that the rider's weight stays where it should be – on their two back seat bones. Remind them of the feel of their stomach and the small of their back going forward, forward, forward in time to walk which is in four-time, with each of the horse's legs moving independently. Explain that trot is in two-time, the legs moving in diagonal pairs, that the movement of their back and stomach will be the same as at walk but quicker and that they will need to lean back slightly more than at walk to feel balanced. They can hold the front of the saddle with their outside hand and lean back slightly against that hand. Their inside hand should be placed in the small of their back and can be thought of as the back of a bench which they should lean back over. Tell them to take just a few steps in trot then to walk again, without collapsing forward as the horse returns to walk. Repeat this until they have the confidence to trot further.

A class lesson may be easier if you have an assistant as leading file who can help to control the pace of the ride and their transitions. The rider's

A rider holding the front of the saddle with one hand. This exercise can also be used when the rider sits into the trot, without stirrups, and still feels in balance and safe.

outside hand will hold the front of the saddle and should be in advance of their inside hand which will be holding the reins in a bridge. They should let their stomach and the small of their back move forward to absorb the motion of sitting trot. Leaning slightly back against the inside hand holding the front of the saddle will help them to stay close to the saddle and feel they are going down into the movement. Their feet should only rest lightly in the stirrups. Repeat on the other rein. To relax the rider get them to say, "Sun-day, Mon-day, Tues-day, Wens-day," to the two-time beat of trot ("Wens-day" is better as it has only two syllables; "Wednes-day" has three.).

To teach sitting trot you must have animals that will trot slowly at an even pace and definitely not a horse which pulls and tries to go faster and faster. A lunge horse should be chosen for its smooth, soft trot. It should be the sort that you would happily ride in sitting trot all day yourself.

On the lead rope or the lunge the rider's outside hand can be on the front of the saddle for them to lean back slightly against and their inside hand can be in the small of their back, palm outwards. Progress to the rider's inside hand hanging down by their sides just behind their seat and just touching the horse's coat, to letting go of the front of the saddle for a few strides at a time until they can manage without holding on with the hand but without gripping with their legs to stay on.

Next, let them have their reins back and begin to control and guide the horse at sitting trot. Practise transitions from walk to trot and walk to halt without the rider losing balance or position. Only when they are good at this should you introduce rising trot.

Unfortunately, in the UK, one of the first questions a beginner is asked is, "Can you do rising trot yet?", as if this is the first and most important achievement – when in fact it is often the start of crouching forward with a rounded back while trying to heave themselves out of the saddle in spite of legs stuck well forward in opposition. Other countries do not have the urge to immediately teach rising trot. I am sure that we should have a re-think on this. I am quite certain that teaching sitting trot first works best and that people taught this way sit better and deeper and have better balance and more confidence and progress quicker.

Rising trot comes easily and effortlessly when introduced later.

How to cross stirrups

Just crossing stirrups with no thought or preparation can leave the rider with a bulky lump of stirrup leather which will painfully bruise the inside of their thighs and make work without stirrups absolute torture.

If you demonstrate how to lift the stirrup leather by the buckle and pull it through and above the stirrup bar – by about 15cm (6in) – before you turn and fold the stirrup leather so that it lies as smooth and flat as possible, your riders will be much more comfortable. Their position will improve far more quickly if they are not in pain.

Lungeing the rider

Riders of any standard from beginner to advanced can benefit from lunge lessons with an instructor who is good at this method of teaching and very experienced in lungeing horses. It is of no help to a rider to be lunged on a horse with a strong actioned, jolty trot. A suitable lunge horse must have a soft, even trot and go in rhythm.

The lunge horse must not be jumpy or nervous and it must answer the command of the person lungeing it smoothly and promptly. Ideally, horse and lunger should know each other well and have complete confidence in each other.

If you don't know the lunge horse it is essential to lunge it first without a rider on to see what sort of temperament it has, what its paces are like and how well it understands your commands.

If you are going to use canter with a rider on you should lunge the horse first at canter without a rider. Many horses which go quietly in trot will

The instructor lunges the pupil with the whip held behind him in the "quiet" position. The horse is going forward freely and the pupil has his right arm in the small of his back, palm outwards. This improves the pupil's body position and encourages him to bring his stomach forward. His left, outside, hand holds lightly on the front of the saddle and his shoulders follow those of the horse. At all times the instructor has his eye on both horse and rider.

give a few bucks when they first canter, then settle down. I would be very wary of using such a horse, other than for very experienced riders, unless this was known to be the horse's normal pattern of behaviour and that it never puts a foot wrong once it has had its "fling".

When lungeing, concentrate 100 per cent. It is only too easy to let the lunge rein get under the rider's inside leg if something makes the horse unexpectedly turn away from you.

If you have not given this rider a lunge lesson before ask how long they have been riding and how many previous lunge lessons they have had. Start them off with reins and stirrups for safety and while they walk and trot on both reins assess their main faults and decide which ones you will work on. If there are several choose two main ones which may affect the whole of the rider's position and work on those. Too many corrections at once are difficult to cope with. Think whether they will be improved more riding with or without stirrups.

Someone who sits hollow backed on their fork, on their "two front seat bones", probably with their bottom sticking out, is going to be made worse if you take their stirrups away.

Someone with round shoulders and a collapsed back is likely to improve more quickly if worked part of the time without stirrups.

Someone wobbly and unbalanced is likely to "grip up" and/or cling on with their calves if you take their stirrups away.

It is probably better not to take reins and stirrups away – novice riders should always have one or the other. Only a very fit and experienced rider benefits from being lunged without holding the front of the saddle with the outside hand and when they have no stirrups. This outside hand is used to hold on to the saddle so that the rider's shoulders are then parallel with the horse's shoulders. Both will carry the outside shoulder slightly in advance. As the rider becomes more confident and their balance improves and they sit deeper in the saddle, just one or two fingers of their outside hand can be tucked under the front of the saddle. This very slight feeling of extra security helps to stop them gripping with their legs when they should be riding by balance. Taking their hand off the saddle is often not a progressive step but a detrimental one because once they develop the habit of "gripping" or "clinging" on they may continue to do so.

Always discuss with the rider what you are doing and why and find out what makes the rider feel better and what makes them feel "wrong". Riders may react quite differently to the same exercise.

Don't go on with the exercise of sitting trot without stirrups for too long with an older or unfit rider or one not used to lunge lessons. A tired rider starts to grip or loses their correct position because their muscles are aching.

Make sure that the saddle is comfortable for that rider. People come in very different shapes and some saddles which slope up abruptly towards the pommel at the front of the seat can be very painful for certain riders. They are often embarrassed to say anything or think it is their fault for sitting wrongly. They may try to sit further back in the saddle or tilt their pelvis back so that the front of their pelvis is not getting bruised.

Lunge lessons in a saddle which is the wrong shape for them can be very uncomfortable for some men. Ask them if the saddle is comfortable.

Some instructors who work riders on the lunge without stirrups to get them deeper in the saddle make the mistake of then lowering their stirrups one or two holes too far. The rider is now reaching down for their stirrups and to do so has to tip forward onto their "front two seat bones", onto their fork. They will now be tipping forward, unbalanced and will not be able to ride as effectively as they did at their shorter length. I am not advocating riding short but I do want to make the point that there is often only one hole's difference between sitting in balance as deep as that particular rider can ride effectively and having them tipping forward unbalanced and completely ineffective. One hole too short is better than one hole too long.

For really quick improvement in a rider there is nothing better than a ten to fifteen minute lunge lesson with a really good instructor every day.

Rising trot

Explain to the pupils the two-time rhythm of trot; that is, the horse's legs move in diagonal pairs. Demonstrate this with two pieces of differently coloured ribbon tied to a diagonal pair of a horse's legs. (Do this with the rider off unless you know the horse well. Some animals, particularly small

Riding faults

A rider rounding his back, tipping forward, and with his toes going down.

A good position for riding rising trot.

ponies which have perhaps never had bandages on, can really panic when they feel something tied round their legs.) Or demonstrate with your own hands and feet.

Being used to the two-time rhythm of sitting trot your pupils will not find it difficult to pick up rising trot. Make sure that they are sitting in balance over their feet and that they have not slid to the back of the saddle with their legs sticking forward. They cannot easily get up out of a chair in this position so they will also find it difficult to rise up out of the saddle. A good saddle, which supports the rider so that they sit in balance over their feet, is necessary if he or she is to learn both to rise effortlessly and correctly.

If the rider's legs are too far forward it is invariably because he or she is sitting too far back in the saddle so the correction is not, "Put your lower leg further back," but, "Sit further forward in the saddle, hitch your seat forward nearer the front of the saddle," then if necessary, "Bend your knee more, lower leg further back." And, "Move your heels back closer to the horse's tail."

All of these are different ways of saying the same thing but one thought will work for one rider and perhaps a different one for another so use more than one way of correcting your pupils. If a rider is consistently behind the movement, sitting to the back of the saddle, legs forward, inspect the saddle. Get the rider to lean right forward with their seat out of the saddle. Lift the back of the saddle as far as possible and, making two fists of your hands, thumbs uppermost, little fingers underneath, put them one on each side under the back of the saddle. Ask the rider to sit down very gently as far forward in the saddle as possible and very gradually put their full weight in the saddle, now supported at the back by your hands. Very often they will now sit comfortably much further forward in what is now, thanks to your hands, the lowest part of the saddle and their legs will naturally fall into the correct position without you saying anything, so that they are now sitting in balance over their feet. This can be an excellent demonstration for the whole class and for the rider to show the importance of a correctly fitting saddle. Just by raising the back of the saddle, thus repositioning the rider's seat and centre of balance, without saying anything as a correction, the rider is now sitting correctly. Let the ride watch you take your hands out. The back of the saddle will sink, your rider will slip back, their back will collapse and their legs will come forward again.

A slight improvement can be made by very carefully and evenly inserting two pieces of foam of exactly the same size and shape under the panel on each side of the back of the saddle to lift it up. They must be absolutely smooth with no lumps or bumps. This should be a temporary measure – the saddle will need re-stuffing.

It is also possible to buy a numnah with a pocket at the back in which a thick wedge-shaped piece of foam can be inserted with the thickest end towards the back of the saddle to lift it up.

Temporarily, a piece of foam can be inserted between the saddle and the numnah. The saddle can then be re-stuffed to fit the horse.

Remember that when the back of the saddle is lifted by more stuffing, the front will come down lower. The rider's weight will be further forward and so the saddle may now press down on the horse's withers. Check this by asking the rider to put their fingers well under the front arch of the saddle while sitting down. Ask them to stand up in their stirrups and lean forward and see if their fingers get pinched. There should still be ample clearance if the saddle is fitted correctly.

To rise to the trot the rider must bring their upper body forward over their knees and think of keeping their feet back as they would when getting up out of a chair. They will find it easier to rise if their balance is a little forward, going with the horse. Their seat should just lightly touch the saddle as they go down and then rise again. They should not make a big effort to rise high but think instead of the horse's stride throwing their hips effortlessly a little forward and a little up.

Common faults in rising trot

1. Rising upright and straight up in the air and throwing the stomach forward at the same time – "high rising". To correct this fault say, "Lean forward a little more and bring your weight forward over your knees. Think of rising forward not up. Let the horse throw you forward and a little up."
2. Being behind the movement and, after rising, sinking heavily down into the saddle often with a collapsed back, then having to make a great effort to heave themselves up out of the saddle again. To correct this say, "Sit further forward in the saddle, put one hand on the front of the saddle and both reins in the other hand. Use the hand on the saddle to keep your seat forward. Bend your knees more, put your feet back closer to the horse's tail. Think of kneeling. Bring your weight further

88   Teaching Riding

forward over your knees and each time your seat goes down just lightly 'touch' the saddle for a second, don't sit down in it."

An effective dismounted lesson for rising trot can be given on a stool of suitable height. The "rider" sits on the front edge of the stool with their feet back underneath them so that they are in balance over their feet. They can then practise "rising" and just touching the stool with their seat. They can improve their balance and accurate body control by rising faster and faster on the stool.

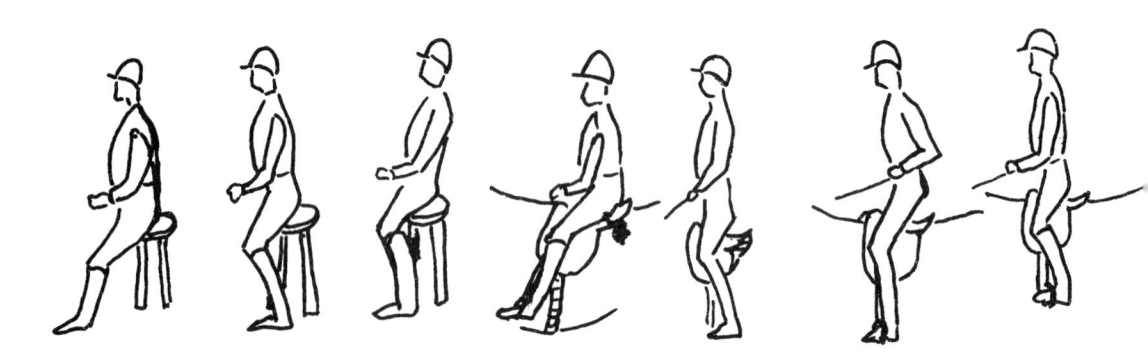

Rising trot. Seven positions, three practised on a stool. These seven positions are a good way of introducing pupils to this exercise: (from left) 1 = very difficult; 2 = easy, good position; 3 = difficult; 4 = very difficult; 5 = high upright, rising; 6 = behind the movement and reins too long; 7 = quite good, but a little too upright.

Try using a stool in this way yourself. It is an intersting experiment and it works!

Changing diagonal at trot

Most people have a favourite diagonal and unless they think about it they will always ride on this diagonal. In the UK it is correct to ride on the outside diagonal when going round a school. That means, trot being a diagonal two-time gait, that the rider's seat goes down into the saddle as the horse's outside foreleg and inside hind leg go to the ground. At first,

Riding faults 89

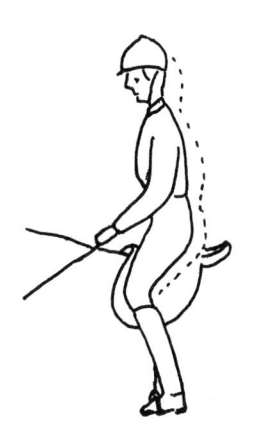

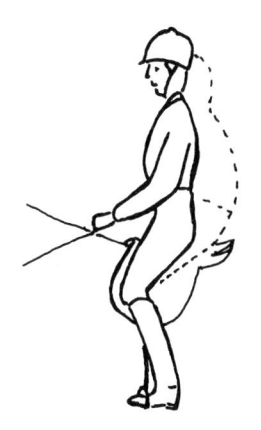

Changing diagonal at trot. Correct (far left), *the rider is just lightly touching the saddle for two beats. Incorrect* (near left), *the rider sits heavily with a collapsed back and is behind the movement. This is likely to make the horse come up above the bit and hollow its back.*

to check which diagonal they are on, the rider has to watch the outside foreleg and shoulder to see if these and their own seat are going down at the same time. As they progress and learn to feel what is happening under them they should know by feel alone which diagonal they are on.

To change diagonal the rider must sit for two beats. Get them to say, "Down, down," as their seat goes into the saddle; then, "Sit, sit," for two consecutive beats. The rider should be on the other diagonal when they rise again.

Get the ride to watch others and see how quickly they can say "Right" or "Wrong". It all helps them to get their eye in and keeps them interested. Many people totally collapse their backs and "Sit, sit" heavily, going behind the movement as they change diagonal. To change diagonal correctly they must stay forward in balance with the horse and just "Touch, touch" the saddle twice as they sit for two beats. Riders who go behind the movement or sit heavily when changing diagonal are likely to notice the horse's head go up and its back go hollow at each change. Watch your ride for this fault and get them to watch each other and note the effect on the horses if done incorrectly.

When teaching rising trot saying the two syllable, therefore two-time, words, "Sun-day, Mon-day, Tues-day, Wens-day, Sun-day, Mon-day," etc., can help the rider and is fun to do and fun to watch as they sit on the first syllable and rise up on every "-day". Adults enjoy this exercise just as much as children do. (Sat-ur-day, Sat-ur-day comes in useful for the three-time beat of canter at a later stage.)

Half-halts or steadying and re-balancing your horse

Beginners at walk round the school can be taught "half-halts". These are often treated as something special only to be taught at a more advanced level but they are just a "steadying and re-balancing" essentially used nearly all the time when riding any horse.

Anyone riding correctly uses half-halts before, during and after changes of direction. They are also used before, during and after changes of gait or pace. They can be a warning to the horse to think and pay attention because the rider is about to ask for something different.

The child at a walk, getting too close to the pony in front, should be told to steady their pony and to sit on their bottom, on their back two seat bones, and ride their pony forward into a "holding hand" (never pulling it back with reins only) to slow it down. This child is performing a half-halt because the pony has slowed down and moved its centre of gravity further back.

Once a rider is learning to steady or turn a horse or is doing changes from one gait to another (transitions) they should be taught half-halts so that these will become a natural habit used all their riding life.

I think the very term "half-halt" sounds complicated, advanced and somewhat mystical. Learning to prepare your horse for something different sounds much simpler. Perhaps we should all keep our teaching simple and easier to understand. Long technical explanations going on for ten minutes are often way beyond riders' understanding and the instructor tends to get bogged down in a sea of technical words. After all doesn't half-halt just mean "think whoa" for a second and anyone can understand that!

Serpentines

Riding a serpentine is an excellent exercise because it teaches riders to change their weight, make alternate use of the reins, use one leg at a time more strongly than the other, use half-halts and recognise when a horse

Bend and control, circles, turns and serpentines. There should be (top) the same amount of bend throughout the neck and body of the horse. Too much bend (below) in the neck and the rider will lose control of the horse's left shoulder. The horse will continue to go to the left, with its head bent too far to the right, and its hind quarters can swing out to the left.

understands their aids (and therefore goes confidently forward) and when it doesn't understand. In the latter case, as the horse approaches the side of the school, its ears go backwards and forwards, its weight changes from left to right, it wavers and is saying to its rider, "Which way do you want me to go? You haven't told me yet and it is nearly too late."

On the turns the horse should be bent to the inside equally throughout its head, neck and body. The outside rein should control the pace and the amount of bend. The rider's inside leg behind the girth should actively prevent the horse falling in and keep it going forward. The outside leg on the girth should be quietly there to control the hind quarters. There should be more weight on the rider's inside seat bone. As it crosses the central AC line the horse should be straight and the rider's weight equally on both seat bones. After crossing the centre line the rider's weight should go more onto the new inside seat bone and the horse should be asked for a bend in the new direction with rein and leg. The inside leg should actively keep the horse out on the required track and keep it going forward.

Adult beginners and tiny children can do this exercise at walk, using six markers to help them guide and control their mounts accurately. I think it is one of the best exercises to work on all-round improvement in a rider. Coordination of aids, change of weight, and rein and leg use come in all the time. A serpentine can be done at walk and sitting trot where the rider has to speed up their reactions and really sit on their back two seat bones and ride their mounts forward.

Serpentines ridden in rising trot are more difficult to ride accurately as riders are not sitting so deep into their horses. It is a good lesson in itself, as there will be plenty of practice of changing the diagonal on the centre line. Ask your ride, after they have ridden a serpentine in sitting and in rising trot, which was the easiest for accurate control of their horse.

Much more advanced riders can do the serpentine in canter, coming forward to sitting trot over the centre line, then changing the bend and aids and asking for canter on the new leading leg. A well-balanced horse and a rider who can coordinate and change his or her aids of weight, rein and leg smoothly but quickly are necessary to do this.

In serpentines, the common fault of dropping the inside hand lower on turns will be obvious. To correct this, the instruction given to the rider as he or she rides on the left rein starting at C could be: "Weight a little more into your left seat bone without leaning your upper body inwards. Left hand up a little to ask for the bend, left leg on to nudge your horse out and prevent it falling in."

As the rider approaches the central AC line, advise them to, "Move more weight into your right seat bone, right hand up to ask for a right bend, right leg nudging your horse to keep it out on the track."

Walk the serpentine yourself with the rider following closely behind you as you give these instructions. That way, it is easier for a class to understand.

Serpentines can be ridden as a ride but riders must be warned to keep out on the same track as the leading file or each animal will cut the turns more and more and the benefit of the exercise will be lost for the riders.

"Keep out, keep out," will be your constant cry – but they must not keep out by using their outside rein which is what will frequently happen.

The exercise of moving the horse over on to the left verge of the road, while looking right to see traffic coming up behind, will help your pupils practise keeping horses out when they try to cut corners.

Serpentine circles (ridden individually)

Instead of riding a half circle in the loop of each serpentine ride a full circle and then continue on the usual track and ride a full circle in the next loop. Using the normal three loops of serpentine the first and third circles will be on the same rein and the second circle on the opposite rein.

8 Canter

Canter is performed in a three-time rhythm, the horse's legs moving in the following order:
1. Outside hind takes the first step of canter.
2. Inside hind and outside fore both together.
3. Inside fore, the "leading leg" because it comes forward in front of the other legs.

Demonstrate this with three different colours of ribbon, one ribbon for the outside hind, two of another colour for the diagonal pair, inside hind and outside fore, and a third colour for the leading leg. Do this with the rider off the horse unless you know the horse well, as an animal which has never had bandages on can panic at the feel of something tied round its legs.

Or demonstrate with your own hands and feet. Do "pretend canter" with the inside leg leading when on a circle. Show this, then show how unbalanced you would be if you "cantered" with your outside leg leading on a circle. It is nearly the same for a horse.

By far the easiest way to teach canter is to go uphill. The rider feels safe because the ground slopes up and therefore the front of the horse slopes up too and the rider is not afraid that they will topple forwards. Riders can be told to lean forward, get their bottom up out of the saddle and take their weight on their thighs, knees and stirrups; with their bottom up out of the saddle they miss the bumping, lurching, disconcertingly strong movement of the saddle and horse under them when they first canter. They immediately or almost immediately feel safe and enjoy cantering. The sloping ground slows the horse down so that it probably voluntarily slows to trot at the top. Holding the mane or a neckstrap at first gives the rider confidence and security.

Just a few steps of canter is sufficient at first so that the rider gets the feel of the movement and realises that the horse is not going to go faster and faster or run away. It will stop of its own accord. Many people have a very real fear that canter is gallop, a fast dangerous runaway gait. You must be aware of this and be sympathetic, understanding and very patient.

On a one-to-one basis, or even two-to-one, as an instructor out on a hack you may be lucky enough to know of a safe suitable slope but the horses must be exceptionally quiet and safe for you to take two canter learners out together.

An enclosed home field may have a suitable slope on which to teach a class to canter. Most likely, however, you are going to have to teach canter in an indoor school or a fenced-in outdoor riding area. It is obvious that riders are more likely to lose their balance on the turn than on straight lines so plan your lesson so that canter starts at the beginning of a long side and the horse trots at the end of that same long side before the corner. Be aware that a rider learning to canter is not going to be able to steady their horse, they will be too busy concentrating on staying on.

If the horses are very used to you and your voice commands they will probably canter on your quick high-pitched voice command, "Can-ter" and trot on your slow, lower-pitched voice command "Trrr-ot". This is ideal and many riding schools have horses which will do this. An alternative is to have a "leading file" who can ride well and whose good mannered, sober horse will control the pace, with your pupil's horse just following.

Obviously, people learning to canter will only do so one at a time. They will have little or no control over their horse so other riders not in your class, or another lesson, should not be in the school at the same time.

Teaching canter sitting forward with the seat out of the saddle definitely works well and gives the rider confidence on an uphill slope. On the level I do not think it is an advantage because the rider then feels that they are going to lose their balance and fall forwards.

When teaching canter in an enclosed area you do need to warn riders about "centrifugal force" – that mysterious power which pulls learner bike riders and learner horse riders off to the outside on corners! They must consciously put a little more weight to the inside. If they have done a lot of sitting trot and learnt this thoroughly so that they have accurate control when in sitting trot and can comfortably and confidently sit to the trot, they will undoubtedly find learning to canter sitting in the saddle easier.

The ardent rising trotters who are still bouncing about at sitting trot are likely to bounce even more at canter. They are also more likely to fall off.

In canter the horse slightly raises its head at one part of the stride and slightly lowers it at another. It is a rocking motion. The rider sits upright, tummy forward as in sitting trot. At the part of the stride where the horse lowers its head they should feel that the whole of the front of their body is stretching out long. They should feel that there is now a longer distance from their waistband to their chin. Both reins should be in their inside hand, so that their shoulders follow the horse's shoulders. They can hold the front of the saddle with their outside hand and lean back a little against that hand as they did when learning sitting trot. Their position will be very much the same but there is this new rocking motion and the feeling of stretching of the front of their body to contend with.

A rider who is competent at sitting trot has the advantage that they are comfortable in the sitting trot used before and after canter. They will not bounce about before, and particularly after, canter when returning to trot as the ardent risers are likely to do.

Only canter one at a time because if there is any problem, say, someone falls off, you do not want the danger of the other horses coming along behind treading on them. Notice which riders are still nervous and only let the people who want to do so try cantering without holding on. Explain that now as the front of the body lengthens and stretches at one part of the stride their hands also follow the movement of the horse's head forward and then their elbows bend more and their hands come closer to their own bodies again as the horse's head comes up. "Your hands belong to your horse's mouth and must follow it," is a saying which can be used very often in teaching riding.

Your riders can now progress to cantering in circles.
1. Learning how to get the horse to lead on the correct inside leg.
2. Learning that asking for canter going into a corner is the easiest place for the horse to get the correct lead.
3. Learning that if their horse just trots faster and faster and finally falls

into canter after the corner they must steady it more before the corner. Their hands must say, "Don't trot fast," and their legs must say, "Come on, canter." (Don't be frightened of using such simple easy to understand words. They usually work better than long technical explanations!)

If the horse does not lead on the correct leg when it usually does with other people, the rider is probably unconsciously hanging on to the outside rein too tightly. This use of the outside rein makes it difficult for the horse to take the correct first step of canter with its outside hind. Because there is not such a strong feel on the inside rein the horse will, in these circumstances, find it easier to start canter with the inside hind and so be leading on the wrong leg.

Many interesting experiments can be done with riders on their feet (and some of them can make instructors think and be more aware than they have ever been before).

Stand square on both feet. Put your right index finger in the corner of the right side of your mouth and pull your head to the right. Which foot is most of your weight now on? It is on your right foot. Which foot would you find it easier to move forward? Your left foot because less weight is on that foot – one reason why canter lead sometimes goes wrong with one rider but not with another rider on the same horse. This also shows that your reins can control or inhibit your horse's use of its hind legs.

To correct this fault in a rider, very often all that is needed is to say, "As you ask for canter push your outside hand forward." This may seem an over-correction but it is a simple thought to follow through and it often works like magic. Keep your ideas and explanations simple.

The aids to canter often cannot come at the beginning of learning because the rider has enough to think about just staying on and not interfering with the horse. Asking for canter going into a corner usually sets up a wise school horse for canter on the correct lead anyway.

Canter aids

With the rider in sitting trot ready to ask for canter, and with the horse's near foreleg leading, the sequence for the required aids for left canter is:

1. Half-halts approaching a corner.
2. Left rein asking for slight left bend.
3. Right rein steadies the horse and controls the amount of bend, but also allows it.
4. Left leg on the girth encourages the horse forward.
5. Right leg behind the girth asks outside hind to take the first step of canter.
6. Weight a little more to the inside, into the left seat bone. This puts weight on the horse's near hind which you *don't want* it to use to start canter. Weight is therefore taken off the outside hind, which frees it and makes it easier for the horse to use that leg with which you *do want* it to start canter.

If the horse, perhaps a little lazy, reverts to trot after a few strides suggest to the rider that it might be because he or she is asking for canter and, when they have got it, thinking, "That worked, it's cantering," – and then doing absolutely nothing else but sit there having a rest so the horse just trots.

Riders should think of every stride of canter as being the first stride. They should ask for canter and continue to ask and ask and ask and ride and ride and ride their horse forward until they can keep the horse cantering as long as they want to. This amount of "asking" will only be necessary on a rather lazy animal.

Which leg is it on?

At first, riders will probably need to glance down to see which foreleg is in advance to know if they have got the correct lead. It may be necessary to lean forward slightly but not to lean right down and hang over the side as many riders continue to do. As they progress and learn "feel" riders should notice that their seat bone, knee and shoulder on the same side as the leading foreleg will feel in a slightly more forward position. They will also feel and can see without bending forward that the horse's shoulder on the same side as its leading leg is slightly more in advance.

If the canter lead is wrong the rider must ride the horse forward to trot and wait until they are approaching the next corner before carefully applying the correct aids again. (Of course, more advanced horses and riders can immediately try again on the straight but then it is much more difficult to get it right.)

Cantering disunited
A horse may break into canter giving a rider a lurching sideways unbalanced feeling.

It may be cantering normally and when the rider suddenly changes balance start to lurch and sway in canter.

It may constantly change from a smooth canter to a lurching, swaying canter on one rein only.

In each case the horse has lost the true rhythm of a three-time canter and its legs are now moving out of sequence. It is cantering disunited.

A horse constantly cantering disunited, or cantering disunited frequently on one rein only, may have back problems. The horse should be examined to see if this is the case.

A rider suddenly changing their balance can make a horse go disunited. If the rider feels this sensation they should immediately ride the horse forward to trot, apply the canter aids for the correct lead and start canter again.

Canter – difficult to get the correct lead
Many horses have a strong preference for one canter lead and some can be extremely difficult to get to lead on the other leg. Very often the off fore is the problem lead.

There are several possible ways of schooling such a horse. One works for one horse, another for a different horse. Two ways are described here.
1. For a placid horse ask the rider to ride in sitting trot on the right rein, with a whip in their left hand. As they go into a corner *with both reins already in their right hand*, right rein asking for a right bend, right leg on the girth, left leg behind it, tell them to use their whip once *exactly* as the left diagonal (off hind and near fore) are on the ground. At this moment the near hind is free to take the first step of canter with off fore leading. (The three-time sequence is near hind, near fore and off hind together with off fore as leading leg). Depending on the horse, the rider

may either need to practise using the whip on several consecutive attempts or the horse may begin to anticipate the whip and canter correctly without the rider using it. (Don't use this method on a nervous or excitable horse as it may become upset.)

2. Put up a pole in the corner of the school. Place a cone at the outside end nearest the corner and raise the inside end about 46cm (18in), or a little more, using a jump stand. The horse wants to start canter with its off hind so that it will have its near fore, favourite, leg leading. If it tries to do that it will knock its off hind on the raised end of the pole. It will be easier for it to use its correct near hind first because this is near the low end of the pole. You will actually see some horses start to use the incorrect inside hind to begin canter, see the raised pole, change their minds and re-start canter correctly with their outside hind leg. The rider must come in to the pole in sitting trot on the right rein with a little more

To solve problems in riding canter to the right, set up a cone, pole and stand in a corner of the school so that the horse approaches on a curve. To encourage the horse to canter with its off fore leg leading, raise the inside end of the pole. Leave the outside end on the ground to help the horse to start cantering correctly, with its near hind leg instead of its off hind leg.

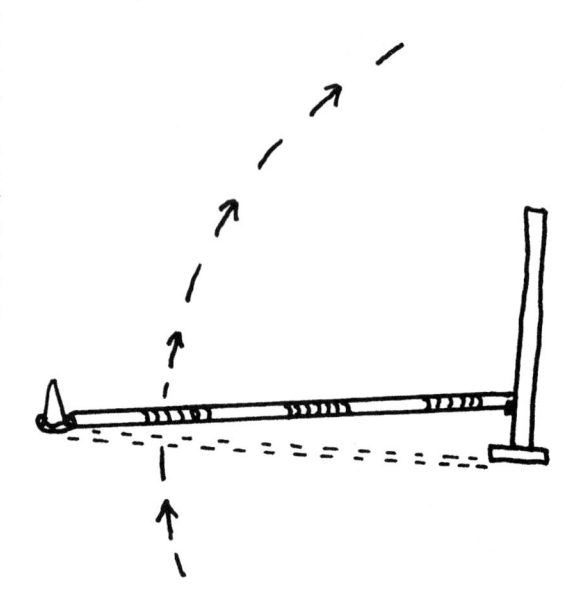

weight in the right seat bone and, exactly at take off, use the aids for canter, with off fore leading. The horse will often have no difficulty in landing in the correct canter lead and the rider must then keep it cantering. Canter a big circle then trot and start canter once more over the pole from sitting trot. Place the pole in different corners. Don't use near fore canter at all. Gradually progress to just a pole on the ground always at a corner, then a mark on the ground made with your heel, or sawdust. Then nothing but still using the corner to start canter.

The advantage of this second way is that the horse does the work. The rider does the preparation so that the method can be used for nervous or excitable horses. There is no pressure and no whip.

When obedience to the off fore canter is well established start to use near fore canter again but to maintain obedience riders must practise their off fore canter more frequently .

Back problems

Notice if someone in your ride looks uncomfortable on their horse on one diagonal in trot. Stand behind the rider when they are in rising trot and see if on one diagonal, instead of being thrown straight forward by their horse, they are being thrown out to one side as they rise and, as they come down in the saddle, they seem to collapse to the opposite side. They will probably say that the horse feels quite different on the other diagonal. This horse may have a back problem.

Other signs of back problems are:
1. The horse constantly goes disunited in canter.
2. It may be reluctant to use the correct lead on one rein.
3. It is very stiff and awkward in a circle on one rein, particularly at canter.
4. Its hind quarters swing out wide on corners as if it has difficulty in bending.
5. When walked or trotted in-hand on a level surface the hoof beats are not in the normal, even four-time beat of walk, or the even, two-time beat of trot. There is a louder stronger beat.

6. The toe of only one of the horse's hind shoes is worn from dragging that toe. (Dragging both toes is usually a sign of weakness, tiredness or laziness.)
7. The horse, standing square and on level ground, when observed from behind may appear to have one hip bone lower than the other and the outline of muscle on one side of the hind quarters may be less pronounced than on the other. A registered equine chiropractitioner or physiotherapist (back expert) may be able to help the horse.

9 Teaching control

Horses rarely go suddenly out of control. Normally, riders gradually lose control by allowing their horses to go into a longer and longer stride of trot or canter, going faster and faster until they are out of control.

Your pupils need to be taught to control their horses in the rhythm of their stride so that each stride is the same length as the stride before.

Steadying and stopping

To steady a horse and keep it at an even pace it may be necessary for the rider to check, check with the reins at every single stride – not pulling or tugging – just a rhythmic feel, feel, feel.

To slow down again the reins must be used in rhythm with the stride, asking the horse to make each stride shorter than the one before. With any horse, but especially a strong, lively horse, teach your pupils to shorten their reins before they start to trot or canter because as they move their hands to shorten their reins during trot or canter a horse that is already trying to go faster will seize that moment when there is less contact on the bit and go really fast.

One of the best ways of controlling a really strong horse is to have quite short reins and put the knuckles of one hand against the horse's neck holding the rein and bracing that hand against the neck (so that the horse is pulling against itself) and then use the other hand to check, check, check with the rein in rhythm with the stride.

A strong horse which pulls the rider and dives its head down is more easily controlled if the reins are held in a "bridge" in both hands – one rein coming into the left hand via the little finger, then going across both hands (with a small gap between the hands) and out via the little finger of the right hand, and the other rein coming in to the right hand lying across the other rein and out through the left hand. The "bridge" on the horse's neck

Control. Reins short, right hand braced against the horse's neck. Left hand steadying the horse in the rhythm of its stride – check, check, checking it to keep each stride the same length as the one before it.

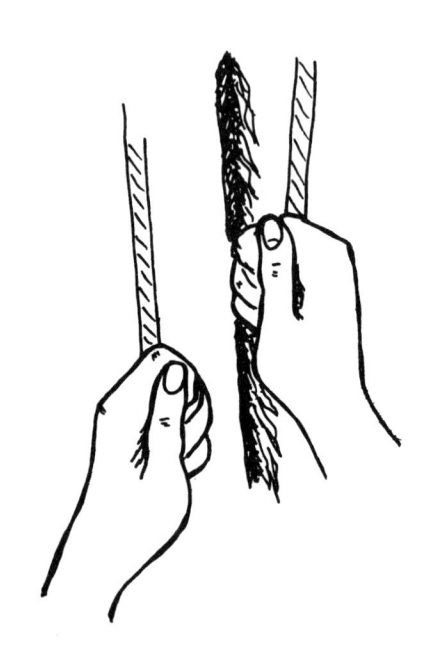

stops the rider being pulled forward out of the saddle and helps prevent the horse getting its head down because it is pulling against itself.

Pulling and tugging, heave and let go, heave and let go will not steady or stop a horse. It is the knack of using the reins in time with the horse's stride that is most effective. It is most important that the rider sits down in the saddle, weight back a little, legs on the horse's sides and heels down, not calves clamped on in a vice-like grip, with heels digging into the horse's sides – which will only make the horse go faster and often causes a horse to take off in the first place.

Practise individually in a ride, shortening and lengthening the stride at trot then at canter. Teach your pupils to feel and work in the rhythm of the stride. The rest of the ride should watch and comment on their successful timing – or not.

Out on a hack (for experienced riders only) ride in a parallel line, with you in the centre. The ride must try to keep level with you as you say to them, "Lengthen stride," at first for only four or five strides, then, "Shorten stride."

Start with trot to make sure that they are all in control then include canter and trot, canter, trot transitions and increase the distances over which you use the lengthened stride.

It is like changing up and down a gear. Riders and horses must learn to stay within the even rhythm of the new gait and feel the rhythm. They must ride smoothly forward into a shortening of stride or a decrease of pace so that the horse's centre of gravity will move further back as it steps under more with its hind legs and it will thus find it easier to slow itself down.

A horse leaning on the rider's hands, head low, back rounded has its centre of gravity so far forward and is so much "on its forehand" that it cannot stop itself. Where possible, turning and riding uphill will help to slow and re-balance the horse to regain control.

Circling, if there is enough space, can help a rider to regain control but they must keep a contact on the outside rein, using the inside rein to turn and the outside rein to help to "neck rein" the horse round. Using both hands on one rein can pull the bit right through the horse's mouth or even pull the horse over. (Explain that if something such as a branch stuck in the horse's tail, an anorak or scarf noisily flapping in the wind, or a box of rattly nails in the rider's pocket have made the horse bolt in panic the rider must get off the second that the horse slows down or it will take off again. It may take some considerable time before it is safe to remount even minus the frightening object.)

For whatever reason, if one of your pupils has been completely out of control but has managed to regain control, ask them to dismount as soon as they have slowed down enough as there is always the danger of a repeat performance. Change the rider or change the horse where possible and avoid the situation which caused the problem in the first place.

Bulging shoulder

Little ponies, their heads pulled firmly round onto their rider's knee, will continue to go fast towards the gate for home or towards other ponies, leading with a bulging shoulder from which their head is turned away. Only their head is turned in the direction in which the rider wants them to go – everything else is going fast in the wrong direction!

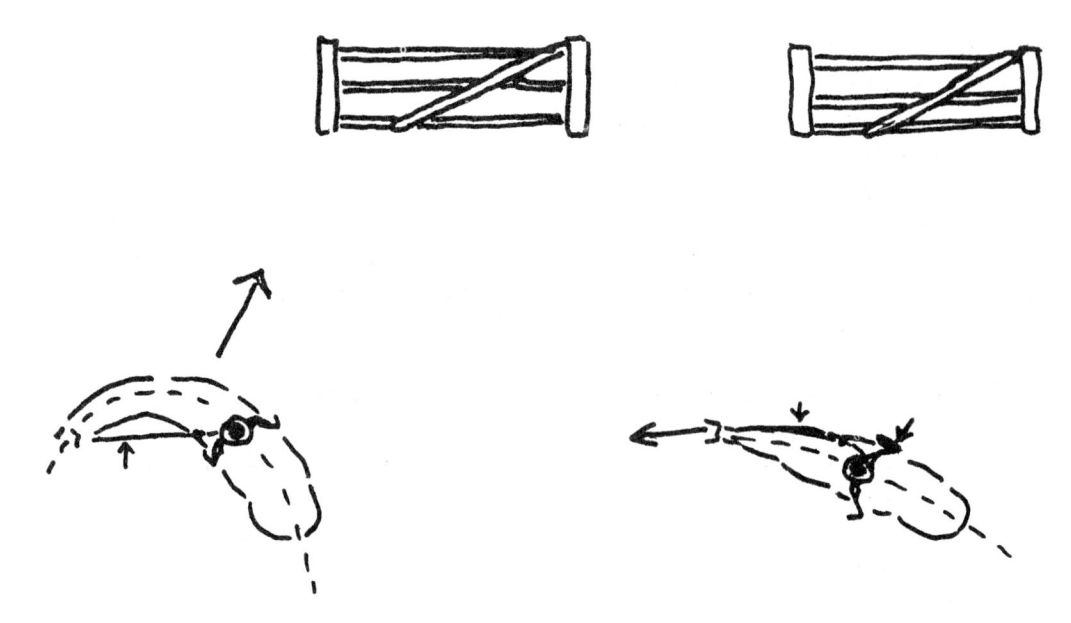

The horse wants to go towards the gate for home and the rider (left) *is using only the left rein. So the horse has bent its neck, bulged its right shoulder and continued to go sideways towards the gate. This rider* (right) *has used the right rein to control the amount of bend in the horse's neck, then used the left rein to guide the horse and at the same time ridden the horse forward with their right leg.*

Horses will also use this ploy to get their own way and a capable rider is needed to correct the problem.

Explain that the rider must think and prepare well before the place where their mount starts to think about arguing and bulging their shoulder.

Say the rider wants to go left and the horse wants to go right. Explain that the right rein must be used strongly to prevent the horse's neck bending to the left. The right rein and the rider's right leg (used forward on the girth) help to control the horse's right shoulder and prevent it bulging out. The left rein is used to indicate the direction in which the rider wants to go but the right rein is in this case the most important rein. Here again, as on so many occasions, it is necessary to remind the rider that, "The faster the horse goes, the more control the horse has, the slower the horse goes the more control the rider has."

So, if the rider is being taken sideways fast tell them to use the right rein (now round the horse's bent neck) to straighten the neck, then both reins, legs and weight to halt. Only then will a smaller or more novice rider have a chance to regain control by using the right rein to control the bend in the horse's neck and the left to indicate which way they want to go. That right rein may need to be used strongly and quite high up the neck (right hand raised) if the horse tries to get its own way again. Lots of leg may be needed too.

The outside rein controls the pace and the amount of bend in the neck. In schooling, hacking, jumping, controlling the horse in any way, correct use of the outside rein is a very important lesson. Some of the occasions when it is needed are:
1. When a horse bends its head and neck and bulges its outside shoulder to get its own way.
2. To keep a horse accurately on a circle.
3. Turning short and sharp into a jump.
4. Asking a horse to go onto a roadside verge and stay on it.
5. Turn on the haunches.
6. Steadying and controlling a horse.
7. Controlling a shying horse.

On the bit

What kind of bit? It entirely depends on the reaction of the horse and the ability of the rider. Probably the majority of horses will be in single joint eggbutt snaffles.

If a horse seems unhappy with its bit through no apparent fault of the rider, the following bits can be tried:
1. Loose ring, wire-ringed snaffle; because the loose rings allow more movement of the bit in the horse's mouth. (Wire rings fit closely into the mouthpiece of the bit and are less likely to trap the lips than flat rings which leave a gap between them and the mouthpiece.)
2. Ordinary cheek snaffle kept in place by keepers on the bridle cheek

pieces. This bit hangs much higher in the mouth than an ordinary single joint snaffle and acts on a different part of the tongue and bars of the mouth. Some horses immediately respond to this different feel by beginning to come on the bit. (The bit must not be too wide for the horse.) The Fulmer snaffle, which has fixed cheek pieces behind which is a fixed bar with a loose ring attached to that, creates a lot of nutcracker action on the lower jaw. This is due to the length between the centre joint and the ring to which the rein is attached. I find there is not enough give or movement in this bit. Also, because of its length, it can push the "V" of the single joint up into the roof of the horse's mouth when the reins are used. This can happen with any cheek snaffle which is too wide for that animal's mouth so the horse opens its mouth from discomfort and the rider then puts a drop noseband on to keep the horse's mouth shut! This happens because the reason for the horse opening its mouth is not thought through.

3. French snaffle. A double-jointed snaffle with a small figure-of-eight shaped section in the centre of the mouthpiece. Many horses go well in this bit probably because there is movement and freedom for their tongue. There is practically no nutcracker action and the action on the lips is softer. This bit can be obtained both as a ring snaffle or as a cheek snaffle so – because of the different height at which they will hang in the mouth and the different parts of the tongue and bars they will act on – both can be tried.

4. Straight bar nylon or vulcanite snaffle. The action of a straight bar bit is different. The stronger use of one rein not only puts more pressure on that side of the horse's mouth but also takes pressure off the other side. This is not so with a bendy rubber snaffle, but some horses chew at a rubber bit. The rider must have very coordinated hands to keep the feeling of riding both sides of the horse's mouth and should be aware of the different action of this bit.

All these bits are allowed in dressage tests when a snaffle must be used.

To successfully teach your pupils how to get their horses and ponies on the bit it is necessary for you to have yourself schooled animals of different types and different temperaments many times and asked this of them.

Unless you have done so, you will not have the knowledge or experience to teach others and the subject is better left. Taught badly it can do more harm than good.

It is easier in a riding school situation where, depending on the level of the school, nearly all or at least some of the horses or ponies should come on the bit, because your pupils can then see and get the feel of what they are aiming for.

In a Pony Club situation you may have to cope with a ride of pupils who have never before tried to get an animal on the bit, and also riding horses or ponies which have never before been asked to do so.

You may be able to work your riders and see a horse going as if, after five minutes' schooling with you on it, it might go forward and down onto the bit for a few seconds. Use it yourself to show the ride what you want them to do. As the ride have ridden circles and serpentines they may have felt their own animals "nod" to the bit for a second before coming up above it again. This is likely to have happened more on one rein than the other because most horses have a preference, so ask your riders which rein they feel is the best for their horse.

To get a horse on the bit its rider must be able to keep their reins in a "straight line" with a constant contact on the horse's mouth so that the rider feels that they "know where both sides of the horse's mouth are" and the horse "knows where both the rider's hands are".

If the rider's reins keep going loose, tight, loose, tight that rider is not ready to ask any horse to come on the bit and it would be unkind to the horse if they attempted to do so. Obviously, if the bit goes from pressing on the horse's mouth to nothing, then to pressing again, the horse will not even have a steady head carriage let alone come on the bit. The rider's hands must be improved first. Unsteady hands can come from an unsteady seat when the rider is not in balance with the horse, or they can come from stiff shoulder and/or elbow joints. This stiffness will prevent the rider's hands from smoothly and accurately following the movement of the horse's head.

Watch their reins in walk (when there is the greatest head movement) and see which riders can accurately follow this movement and maintain a contact on their horse's mouths.

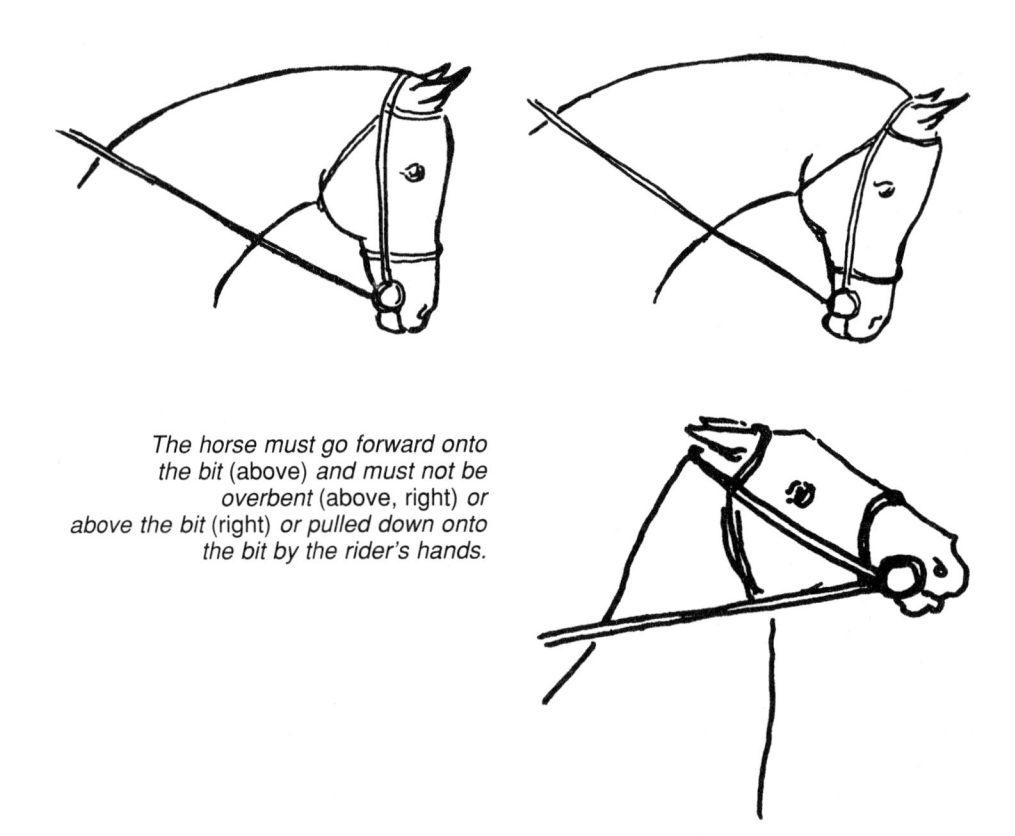

The horse must go forward onto the bit (above) *and must not be overbent* (above, right) *or above the bit* (right) *or pulled down onto the bit by the rider's hands.*

It is probably easiest to teach riders to get a horse on the bit at walk but explain that the horses must be ridden forward into the contact of the rider's hand and not pulled back (which will shorten their stride in walk), nor brought onto the bit by just dropping their heads and bending their necks without stepping under from behind.

A tiny movement of the rider's fingers to move the bit on one side of the horse's mouth or the other (but so small a movement that it cannot be seen) may encourage the horse to relax its lower jaw and when ridden forward come down on the bit. The tiny movement should be on whichever side of the horse's mouth it responds to best while learning. The movement must not be on one side of the mouth then the other, left, right, left, right. Unfortunately, this is often seen at all levels of riding – and even more unfortunately, pupils are quite often taught to do this.

This ugly movement will only, incorrectly and in a false outline, bring the horse down onto the bit from in front.

The horse may develop a left, right swing of its head from the rider's alternate use of reins and it may also develop a "broken neck" (an incorrect bend halfway down the neck instead of the correct bend at the poll).

At first, horses will be on the bit, nodding their heads for just a second in a whole circle. Gradually, they will come down for longer and come down more often during the circle. The horse must be given time to understand what the rider wants and must accept the bit without stiffening against it which is what will happen if the rider is impatient, too demanding with their hands or not using enough leg.

The same thing can be tried on the other rein when the horse will stay on the bit for most of the circle on what has been chosen as its best rein. Frequently give the horse time to stretch its neck out and down to rest its muscles which are perhaps unaccustomed to this work. When the horse can do a full circle on the bit on both reins it is still likely to come above the bit when the rider changes rein. The reason for this is that when the rider changes rein their weight in the saddle changes, their hand position changes and their legs too alter position. Very few riders can at first coordinate all these movements so that they happen so smoothly and gradually that there is no sudden difference, however slight it may be. The horse may not be ridden forward sufficiently into an even hand contact, it may not be kept between leg and hand and held carefully and accurately enough so it comes up above the bit during the change of rein.

When the horse will stay on the bit throughout a figure-of-eight at walk the whole process can be tried in trot. Should it be done in rising trot or should it be done in sitting trot? I don't think there is a hard and fast rule. It depends on the rider. It depends on the horse.

Obviously, if a rider is a bit jolty and unstable in sitting trot their horse will not stay on the bit because its rider's hands will have an uneven contact on the horse's mouth. Such riders are not really ready to ask the horse to come on the bit but they may be able to keep an even contact in rising trot. If so let them use it – but work to improve their sitting trot also.

Some horses go forward better and stay "round in outline" better when their rider is in rising trot – so use it. Others can be kept on the bit better by their riders riding them strongly forward in sitting trot. See which works best for each horse and rider partnership, discuss it and discuss the probable reasons. It is interesting to riders to watch other horses in their own ride work so that they can actually see when horses come down onto the bit and notice when and why they come above it.

Keeping the horse on the bit while changing the rein at trot is even more difficult than at walk because there is more movement. Here the sitting trot rider is perhaps at a slight advantage because they do not have to move as much as the rising trot rider who might feel the necessity to change diagonal as they change rein. Keeping the horse on the bit in rising trot during a change of diagonal really does test the rider's ability to sit absolutely in balance and just touch the saddle lightly twice in changing. If this action of changing diagonal always causes the horse to come up off the bit during a change of rein then don't change diagonal. Ride one whole figure-of-eight or serpentine on one diagonal and the next on the other, then practise changing diagonal in a straight line until the rider has got it right and the horse is not unsettled by it. Only then try again changing at the normal places.

When going into canter on the bit the hands must have enough contact to keep the horse on the bit but give enough to allow canter. The horse must be ridden forward into the first stride of canter and the rider must continue to ride it forward at every stride of canter. To keep the horse on the bit a delicate balance between leg and hand is needed.

Transitions down

Here is where nearly all early dressage test sheets say, "Above the bit, resisted into trot, walk or halt." Probably more difficulty is found in keeping horses on the bit in transitions down than at any other time. Nearly always it is for one of the following reasons:
1. The rider uses too much hand.
2. Their hands stiffen.
3. Their hands go lower and push downwards.
4. Their shoulders and elbows stiffen.

5. The amount of pressure on the bit suddenly alters.
6. The transition is asked for from front to back instead of forward from back to front.
7. The horse is insufficiently warned and prepared by preliminary half-halts.
8. Not enough leg is used to ride the horse forward into the transition – yes, even forward into halt.
9. The transition down has always been asked for at a marker instead of practising with the priority being a transition down, on the bit, done anywhere but with no resistance.

Don't teach transitions down at a marker until riders can achieve them without resistance when given a free choice of where they are to occur.

If horses either come heavy on their forehands or come above the bit on transitions down ask their riders to gradually bring the horse onto a circle, then smoothly onto a smaller circle so that the circle brings the horse into a transition down and the riders feel this happening smoothly and effortlessly. The circle makes the horse step under more with its inside hind leg and so move its own centre of gravity further back which makes the downward transition much easier.

How long will it take to get a horse on the bit? How long is a piece of string? It depends on the horse and rider. It depends how often they school and whether they make calm, steady, thoughtful, gentle progress or whether, on just one day, they get impatient or aggressive and undo all their good work and so have a long setback. Give them this advice: "If you feel cross and over-tired, or if you have had a row with your mother, father, boyfriend, husband, don't school your horse – go for a quiet hack instead."

Turn on the forehand

This is a useful exercise because it teaches the rider accurate control of the horse and makes them think and feel what is happening under them.

Make it simpler for the horse and rider by asking them to ride straight at a fence, hedge or wall of the school. First, they must have their reins

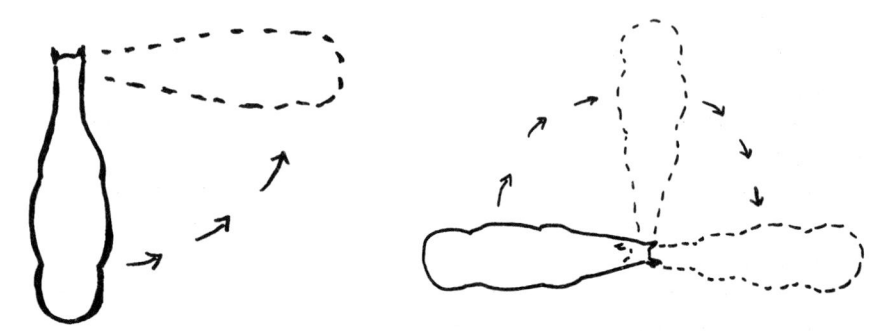

When the horse is asked (left) *to make a quarter-turn to the left its hind quarters will go to the right, away from the rider's left leg. And, if asked* (right) *to make a half-turn to the right on the forehand, its hind quarters will go to the left.*

short enough so that they do not halt and then immediately start reefing in their reins. Facing a barrier the horse cannot go forward. The rider must keep the horse's forehand in the same place with their reins and ask it to move its hind quarters over with the legs. If the horse is to be asked to do a quarter-turn to the left its hind quarters will go to the right away from the rider's left leg.

The horse will want to step forward to the left with its forelegs so the rider must anticipate this and check the horse gently with their right rein. They must not use their left rein or the horse will step forward. This rein is just to get a slight left bend so that the rider can see the horse's eye. Their left leg behind the girth nudges gently asking the horse to move its hind quarters over towards the barrier (crossing its near hind over its off hind as it steps sideways). The rider's right leg on the girth controls the speed and number of the horse's sideways steps. The forelegs are picked up and put down within the same small area. The aids must be gentle, and particularly when teaching a horse, only one step at a time should be expected. The rider must not be rough or aggressive with their aids or the horse will step forward then back, become really agitated and cease to "listen to the rider" or to try to think what the rider is asking it to do.

The rider must think and feel what is happening under them. If they feel the front of the saddle come up a fraction that is a signal that the horse is about to take a step forward so they must very gently check it with their right rein. If the back of the saddle comes up more the horse is about to step back so the rider must gently close both legs to stop this happening. When the horse's body is very nearly parallel to the barrier the rider must put their right leg on the horse's side more strongly and ride it forward the first few steps from their right leg. If this is not done the horse's hind quarters tend to collapse outwards to the right, because they are still moving away from the rider's left leg.

Most riders use far too strong aids and have an agitated horse stepping backwards then forwards not knowing what they want. Take it slowly, quietly and gently one step at a time. If anyone is getting no reaction at all go to them, hold the horse's cheek piece in your left hand and with your right hand in a "fist" gently try to nudge the horse over a step at a time. Praise the rider, who must praise the horse for any reasonable attempt. When quarter-turns are progressing well in both directions try half-turns.

Here the rider halts on an inside track (to leave room for the horse's head to turn) parallel to a fence, wall, hedge or barrier. They are now doing two quarter-turns consecutively in the same direction and it is as the first quarter-turn is almost completed that the rider must be aware that the horse now sees an inviting gap to step forward into. As the horse starts to come at right angles to the barrier the rider must use the rein which is not asking for the bend to check the horse gently and prevent it stepping forward. Again, as the half-turn is nearly completed and the horse's body is almost parallel with the fence, the rider must ride forward, at first with the leg nearer the barrier to prevent the hind quarters collapsing.

Turn on the haunches

To be correct the turn on the haunches should be done from walk keeping rhythm throughout and continuing in walk. If neither horse nor rider have done this before it is easier to start from halt. The reins must be short enough before they begin.

The pupils ride the horse on the left rein at walk deep into a corner and halt when the horse's hind quarters are as near to the corner as possible, using a little more right rein to halt the horse. Their right leg and the right

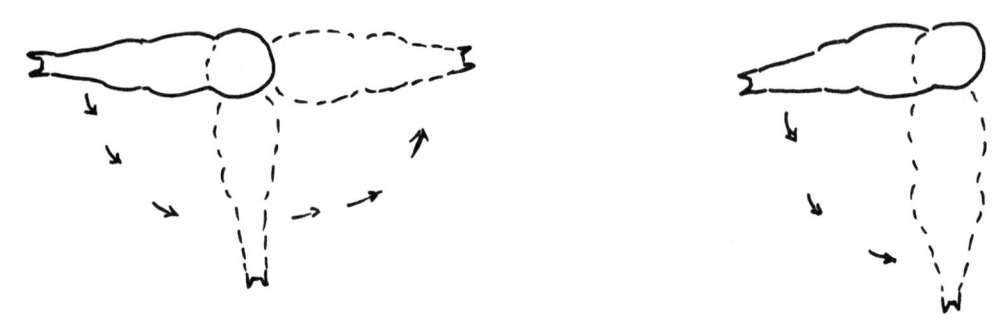

Making turns to the left on the haunches: (left) *a half-turn; and* (right) *a quarter-turn.*

rein control the horse's off (right) hind leg which is the one that the horse is going to want to step sideways with. The rider's lifted hands are carried a little to the left, so that the right rein presses lightly on the horse's neck, still keeping the right hand on the off side of the neck. The right leg, still – but holding strongly behind the girth – prevents the horse's hind quarters swinging out to the right. The left leg, still – on the girth – is ready to be used with the right leg if the horse steps back. The rider can think "up and over" in front with hands and body as they put a little more weight into the left seat bone. The aids are very light and gentle.

Most horses find this exercise easier than the turn on the forehand. A horse will soon respond when its rider asks for a half-halt, begins to change his or her weight and thinks "up and over" with the forehand. Horses which step back usually do so because the rider uses the reins far too strongly. In turn on the haunches the forelegs cross over each other. The hind legs keep the rhythm within the same small area.

Progress to keeping the same rhythm of walk approaching the corner and during the quarter-turn. When practising half-turns think of them as two quarter-turns. Too much rein will make the horse back into the barrier or wall as it finishes the first quarter-turn of the half-turn.

Rein back

When opening gates and for avoiding dangerous situations, rein back is essential. Very often horses and ponies are seen being hauled in the mouth, while the rider kicks with their legs. No wonder the animals so often stand there open-mouthed. "Stop with the reins, go with the legs. What does this rider want me to do?" An excitable horse may start to do little rears.

A horse can be taught to rein back from the ground and this exercise can be usefully done in a ride because it is often necessary to make a horse back when a person is on their feet or when the horse is standing on their foot!

Stand in front of the horse, facing it. Put one hand on the bridge of its nose and the other on the point of its shoulder. Put a toe on the coronet of the foreleg that is more forward and press on it. At the same time push back with both hands and say, "Back," in a distinctive deep voice that the horse will recognise again. When it takes a step back, press a toe on its other coronet, push on its nose and shoulder and say, "Back." Then walk it forward. Halt and do it again.

The mounted horse is helped to keep straight in rein back if a pole is dropped on the ground parallel to a wall of the school, or if out in a field beside a fence, to form a passage. In the open, two poles can be used to form this passage.

The rider must have their reins short enough before they start. It is no good halting then reefing in the reins and pulling on them. With short enough reins, tell them to ride into the passage and ask for halt towards the end of the passage, by closing both legs on the horse's side and riding it forward into a holding hand. Instead of easing the reins as in a normal halt they keep the contact on the horse's mouth, keep the legs quietly holding its sides, move the fingers a little so that the bit presses, moving a little in its mouth, and say, "Back," in the usual way. Tell them to have their seats a little lighter in the saddle to make it easier for the horse to raise its back behind the saddle in order to take a (two-time in diagonal pairs) backwards step.

If necessary an assistant can stand in front of the horse pressing on its coronets in turn and with their hands on nose and shoulder pushing it back. After two or three steps back the rider should ride the horse forward into an ordinary halt so that it will not get into the habit of running back when asked to halt.

If the horse swings its hind quarters sideways it must be corrected by the rider's leg pushing it straight again. The rider's leg correction in rein back is pressing its side not nudging because nudging is asking for forward or forward and sideways movement. The rider's legs are quiet, not active, when asking for rein back.

To rein back an exactly accurate number of steps, say four steps, teach pupils to ride their horse forward again as the horse begins to take the fourth step so that it will back onto that diagonal pair of legs and then immediately step forward.

10 Saddlery

Martingales

Neckstraps are a good idea when teaching and all martingales have them (except the Irish which is mostly used for racing and is just two rings joined by leather to keep the reins together).

Running martingales

When fitting a running martingale "stops" should always be used on the reins between the martingale rings and the bit; these stops will prevent the rings catching. There should always be a stop where the martingale and neckstrap meet. The martingale itself should be attached to the girth so that the rings reach up into the horse's throat when its head is at the normal angle. Some books tell you that the rings should reach back to the horse's withers but this does not give an accurate fitting as it depends on the size of the horse's shoulder – which is not where the martingale is worn anyway!

Standing martingale

The standing martingale should be fitted so that, when it is attached to the girth and a cavesson noseband, the loop should reach the horse's throat.

The disadvantage of the standing martingale is that, whereas a running martingale teaches a horse to improve its head carriage and can often be dispensed with, a standing martingale often teaches a horse to lean against it. The horse then develops a large bulge of muscle under its neck and often becomes ewe necked. The standing martingale may help to control a horse which throws its head up but it does not improve the horse.

Market Harborough

A martingale which does improves the horse and also gives the rider more

A running martingale correctly fitted and with safety "stops" (arrowed) on the reins.

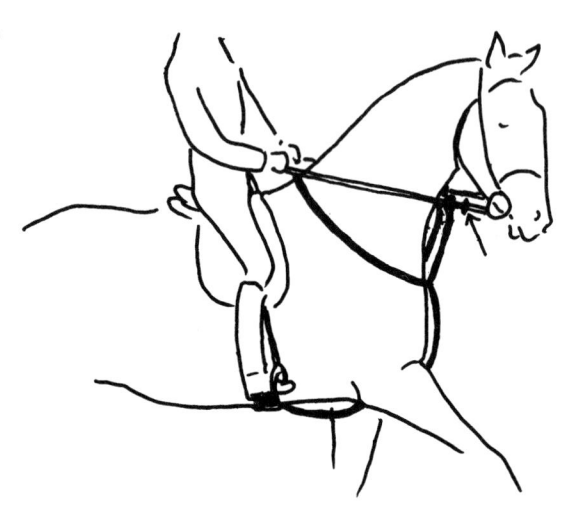

control is the Market Harborough. The reins of the Market Harborough have three or four "Ds" on each side at different lengths for adjustment, and this martingale fits on to the girth and through the neckstrap loop as the others do. It then divides into two straps with clips at the end. These pass through the rings of a snaffle bit from inside to outside and onto the special reins.

The Market Harborough should be adjusted so that when the horse's head is at a normal height the rein comes into action on the bit just before the Market Harborough straps which pass through the bit. It only works when the horse puts its head up and its action is to ask the horse to bring its head down again. The horse can stretch its neck forward and out so the Market Harborough can be used for jumping. The rider cannot use it severely (if correctly adjusted) because it is the horse which makes it work. When introducing it to a horse for the first time use it with an ordinary rein as well and tell the rider to push their hands forward to take pressure off the horse's mouth if the horse runs back as this will immediately stop the martingale working.

Very occasionally, horses are upset by a too sudden introduction to the Market Harborough. Usually they go exceptionally well and horses build

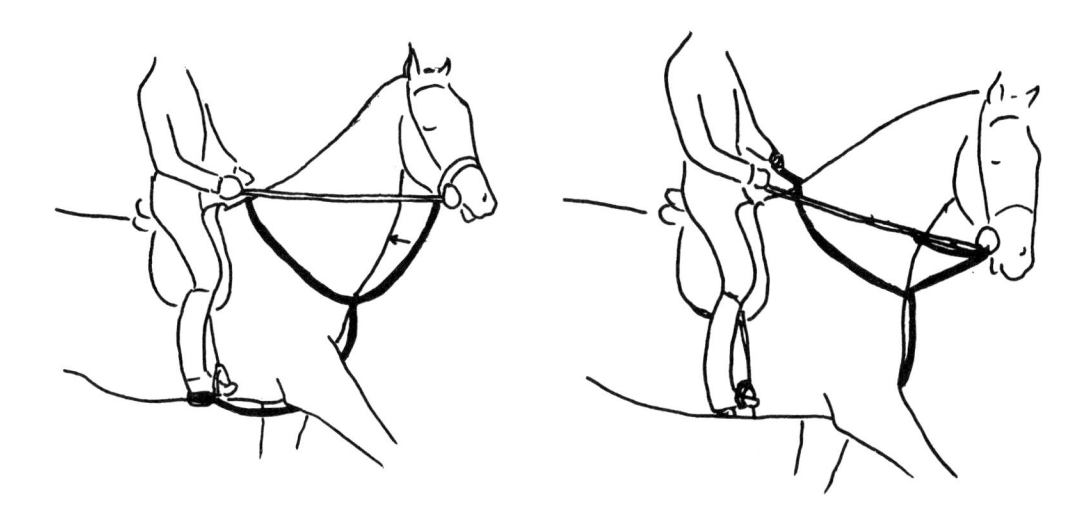

Horses that are fitted with a standing martingale (left) often develop a ewe neck and a bulge of muscle (arrowed) in their lower neck, The Market Harborough (right); the ordinary rein should come into contact just before the Market Harborough.

up muscle on top of their necks and improve their top line. Riders get a light feel of a horse going in a correct outline.

As the horse improves the Market Harborough can be dispensed with or only used occasionally. It does help a child or weak person to control a stronger animal.

Some horses may learn to "lean" on the Market Harborough and become "heavy" in which case stop using it.

Nosebands

Nosebands done up too tight can cause sore places where they pass over the sharp protruding bones on each side of the horse's bottom jaw. The correct height is two fingers below the projecting cheek bone.

Cavesson nosebands fitted too low can cause the horse's lips to be pinched between the bit and the noseband when the rider has a contact on

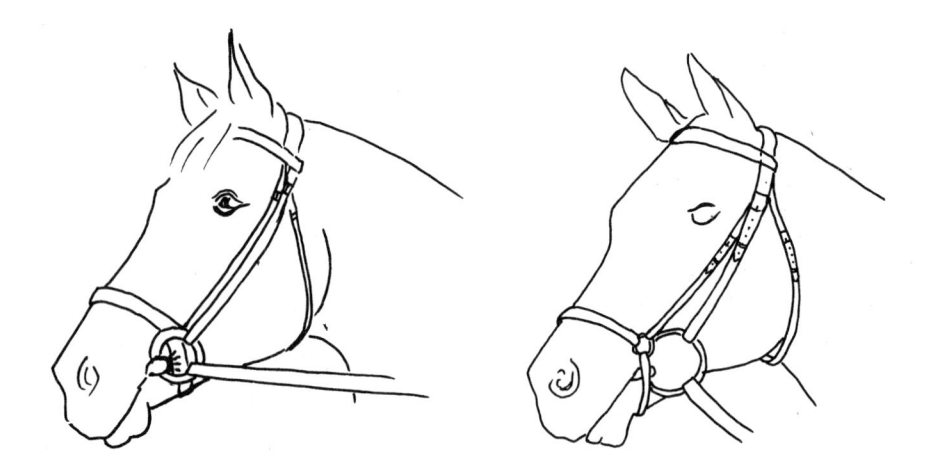

A cavesson noseband (left) fitted too low. When the reins are used the horse's lip will be pinched between the bit and the noseband. Very painful for the horse and often not noticed until the damage is done; a correctly fitted drop noseband (right); the bit is well positioned. and the noseband is placed high enough to be well clear of the horse's nostrils.

the reins. This action of the reins lifts the bit in the horse's mouth and so traps the lip, sometimes making it bleed.

The rider is often unaware of this pinching because, with no contact on the reins, when tacking up for instance, everything seems comfortable. Check for this problem.

Drop nosebands

To accept the bit a horse must be able to relax its lower jaw. It cannot do this if a drop noseband is done up like a girth. Most horses will resent the discomfort of a very tight drop noseband. A drop noseband that is low can interfere with a horse's breathing if the noseband is down on the soft part of the nose below the hard bone which runs down the front of the horse's face.

Flash nosebands

A flash noseband should be made of strong, solid leather thick enough to prevent it sagging down in front where the flash strap is attached.

Nosebands which have sagged down in front often interfere with the horse's breathing because the flash is done up tight round the lower, soft part of the nose instead of being up on the bony part.

Double bridle

Before using a double bridle your pupils must learn to accurately handle and control two pairs of reins. An ideal way of doing this, without the possibility of upsetting a horse, is to put a second pair of reins on their snaffles. It does not really matter if both pairs are not exactly the same length as those on the double bridle should be. (Make sure the second pair are not so long that the loop could slip round the rider's foot.) It is more helpful to the rider if the reins are of different widths; the thinner reins can be attached to the bit below the others and be thought of as the "curb rein". By look and feel it should then be easy for the rider to tell one from the other.

The top "bradoon" controlling and guiding rein is held either outside the little finger or between the little finger and the third finger. The narrow

Practise first (left) *with two reins on a snaffle bit before* (right) *fitting a double bridle.*

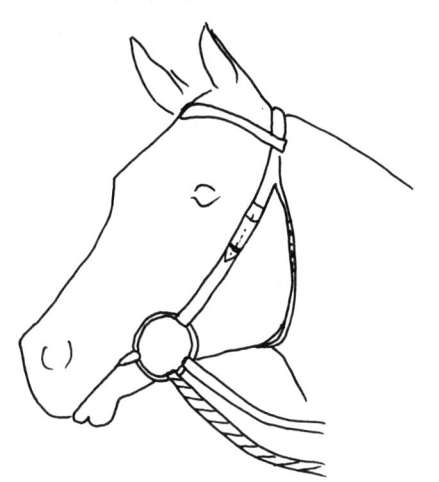

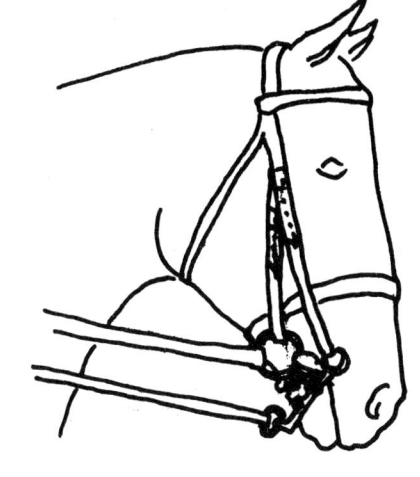

bottom "curb" rein is held either with one or two fingers between it and the bradoon rein. In some countries, France for instance, it is usual to have two fingers between the reins of a double bridle. This has the advantage of enabling the rider, by altering the angle of their wrist, to have a little more or a little less curb action without altering the length of their reins.

Because the bradoon rein is held lower in the hand (which should be in the normal thumbs on top position) than the curb rein, when viewed from the side the reins cross over each other.

The curb rein asks the horse to flex at the poll and relax its lower jaw. It is not a "brake" though it is often thought of as being one. Its severity comes from two sources:

1. The length of the cheek of the curb bit which acts as a lever (in conjunction with the curb chain). The longer the cheek is above the mouthpiece the greater the leverage on the poll (where the bridle passes over the top of the horse's head). The longer the cheek below the mouthpiece the greater the leverage on the bars of the mouth.
2. The tightness of the curb chain. Old photographs of riders eighty to ninety years ago show that they rode (and jumped out hunting) in very long cheeked double bridles. They must have had very good, light hands and been very confident that they would not jab their horses in the mouth when jumping. Double bridles were thought of as normal and correct turnout. Children as young as ten years old rode and jumped in double bridles with two pairs of reins and none of the devices to make two reins into one as often seen today. It is possible that giving up regular use of double bridles has made hands less sensitive and seats less independent nowadays.

Fitting the bits

The bradoon should be fitted as a snaffle is. The curb should fit the width of the horse's mouth comfortably so that there is no sideways pressure on the lips and the lower part of the bit cheeks are clear of the lips. It should lie just below the bradoon in the horse's mouth. When the bridle is on the horse will, with its tongue, lift the joint of the bradoon up and over the curb bit so that it now rests on top of it. The smooth curb bit, with its raised port to allow room for the tongue, now rests directly on the tongue and on the bars of the mouth. The bradoon headpiece should do up on the off side of the bridle.

Fitting the curb chain
1. When the curb chain is attached to the off side curb hook by the top of its first link, twist the curb chain clockwise until it is flat. Make sure that the little central fly link is hanging down from the bottom of the chain.
2. Attach the top of the last link of the curb chain to the near side curb hook.
3. Attach the bottom of the link which is at the correct fitting (45 degrees) to the near side hook. (The reason for doing it in this order is that if you need to alter the length of the curb chain you do not have to release the whole thing.)
4. Thread the small leather lip strap which is attached to little "Ds" at each side of the curb bit through the fly link. This was once used to prevent the old-fashioned very long-cheeked curb bits from flipping upside down. The lip strap also helps to keep the curb chain in place. After riding in a double bridle check where the curb chain presses over the two boney projections of the lower jaw as it can rub and make sore places. A rubber curb guard can be slid over the curb chain to protect the jaw if necessary.

When correctly fitted the curb chain should come into action when the cheek of the curb bit is at 45 degrees to its normal position.

It is absolutely essential that riders using a double bridle can control their reins so that each rein on the left is held at the same length as its corresponding rein on the right. By the length at which they hold their reins the rider must be able to regulate accurately the amount of curb action that they want and be able to maintain this length. People are often seen riding with one curb rein tight and the other side hanging down in a loop and they are totally unaware of this. There should be more contact on the bradoon than on the curb with most horses.

When your pupils can cope with two pairs of reins accurately you may notice a definite improvement in the sensitivity of some, if not all, of their

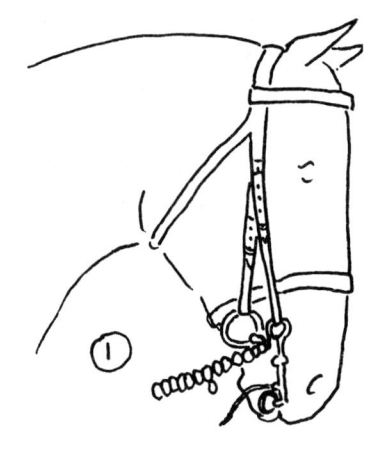

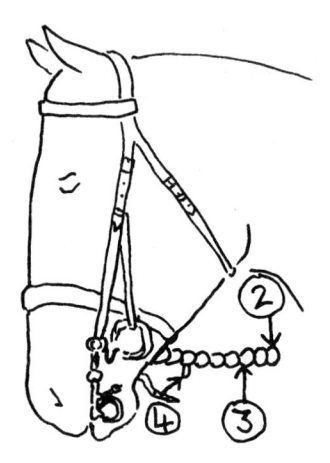

Fitting the curb chain. 1) Attach to offside curb hook and twist clockwise until smooth. 2) Attach top of last link of chain to nearside curb hook. 3) Attach the bottom of the link which is at the correct fitting (45 degrees) to the nearside hook. 4) Thread the lip strap through the fly link and do it up.

hands. For this reason riding with two pairs of reins is an excellent exercise in itself. They have to concentrate and think about their hands so it is very good for the "ham fisted", strong handed or rough rider.

When a horse is first introduced to a double bridle it should be fitted with a looser curb chain and be hacked out quietly or ridden in a school on a loose rein a couple of times to get used to the feel of the two bits in its mouth before being schooled in it with a correctly adjusted curb chain.

Most horses go extremely well in double bridles if they have an educated rider. A double bridle is the most versatile because:
1. It can be as mild as a snaffle if the curb rein is not used.
2. It can ask for a flexion with most delicate aids if the curb rein is used.
3. The lever action of cheek and curb chain (and pressure on the poll) can be used as mildly or as strongly as necessary.

Once an experienced rider has become really familiar with riding horses in double bridles they will know that they are the equivalent of playing a musical instrument. There is infinite choice of how to use each part to suit each horse or to get different reactions from the same horse. They are fascinating and an education in themselves and so worth far more use and thought than is now given to them.

Ride in a double bridle as often as possible yourself and try to introduce your pupils to the feel of riding a horse in a double bridle. So often they are just used to teach BHS exam candidates or riding club/Pony Club test candidates the minimum required to pass and then never used again.

11 Lessons using barrels or cones

Just going round in a school or riding area day after day, leading file to the rear and doing turns, circles and serpentines can be incredibly boring for horse and rider.

Try putting eight large barrels in two rows 6m (13yd) apart in each direction (large cones will do but barrels are better because they are solid enough to make the horses respect them).

You can ride so many patterns with these barrels that there is never a dull moment. The horses understand what is being asked of them because there is something to go round or in and out of. The riders really try to ride accurately because they and everyone else know if they have not succeeded in guiding the horse accurately. The whole ride have to think and be accurate. The whole ride have also to be involved in the task most of the time. If barrels are used everyone knows if they have been lazy and let the horse get too close because there is a noise when their foot hits the barrel!

It is more fun, pupils work harder and learn more and they and the whole ride know when they have succeeded, improved or failed. There are innumerable ways of using the barrels.

Here, I suggest ten ways which are fun to do and instructive for both horse and rider:
1. Circles – three possible ones.
2. Changes of rein.
3. Figure-of-eight.
4. Bending singly or in pairs and going straight after one row of bending.
5. Butterflies – round the outside end two barrels (one wing), inside the middle two barrels, outside the other end two barrels (the other wing).
6. Serpentines round two barrels and straight across the centre, etc.
7. Egg timer serpentines round two barrels and diagonally across the centre.

8. Circling round the barrels and staying on the same rein.
9. Circling round the barrels and changing the rein.
10. Cogs in two wheels.

There are endless possibilities and I am sure that you will think of more yourself. Teaching with barrels is great fun and is really enjoyed by pupils of all ages. Try it!

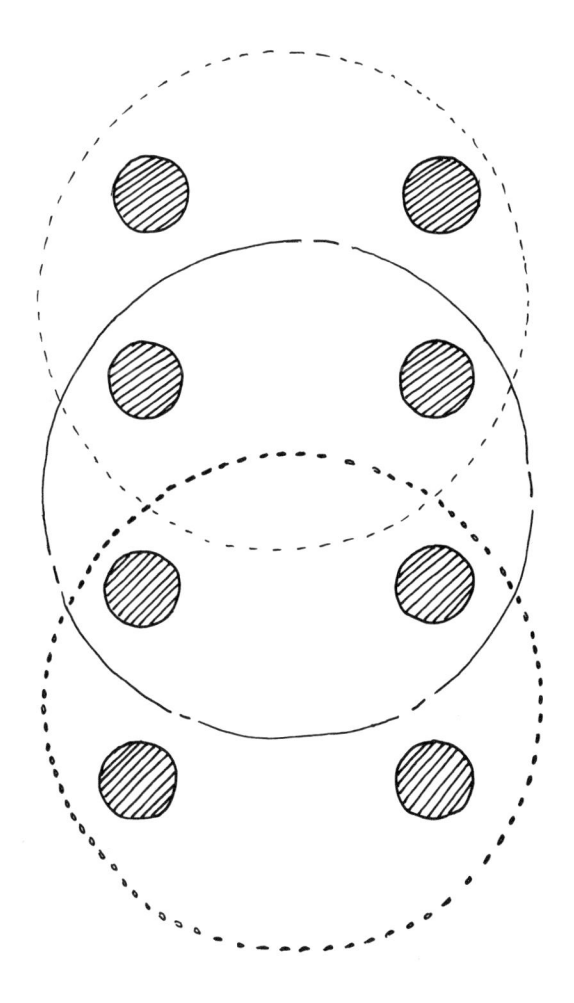

A formation of eight barrels which can be used for different circles, figure-of-eights, bending and so on. The variations are innumerable.

By increasing the size of area used and increasing the number of barrels or cones you can keep a large class occupied, interested and learning with this method.

Riding in traffic

When preparing pupils for riding in traffic, it is best to start practising at home, either in the school or in a field.

Riders must become competent enough to move their horses sideways onto the verge or into the side of the road with their horse's head facing away from the direction of movement. In the UK, when a ride is on the left side of the road the horses will be looking right and moving away from their rider's right leg.

The horses look to the right in order to see traffic coming up behind them. Because it is natural for a horse to keep its eye on something that it is not sure of, it is essential that it sees the traffic behind with its right eye. If the horse is frightened by a vehicle it will keep its right eye on the vehicle and if it does swing its hind quarters they will go away from the traffic towards the verge. If the horse sees traffic with its left eye and keeps its eye on it, its hind quarters will swing out into the road and could be hit by the vehicle.

Practise at home first. Teach your ride to come on an inside track on the right rein and to steady their horses with their left rein. Then ask them for a right bend so that they can just see the horse's eye, then change their forward movement to forward and sideways by keeping the right bend, checking the horse with their left rein, then using their right leg behind the girth to nudge the horse over.

Riders must think and feel the rhythm of "check and step over" as the horse moves forward and sideways onto the track. This movement is called leg yielding, which perhaps makes it sound both high powered and difficult. However, when a horse shies sideways away from something it naturally performs this movement so horses do not find it difficult.

Get the ride to do leg yielding on both reins but, of course, making sure every one understands that knowing how to move their horses over to the left while bent to the right is the priority for riding in traffic.

Lessons using barrels or cones   131

If you have a young horse out, or one that is a little frightened of traffic, place it in a pair with a very steady horse between it and the traffic; and have quiet horses in front and behind if possible. If there are only three horses in all, have one quiet horse in front of the frightened horse and one beside it; it is easier to control a horse which wants to shoot forward

This rider (left) *has used the left rein. The horse shies out into the path of the traffic. The horse's right shoulder escapes. With its left eye, the horse sees traffic coming up behind it. Very many road accidents are caused in this way, the horse being hit in the hind quarters by traffic coming from behind. Here* (right) *the rider is using the right rein, right hand raised to control the horse's shoulder by keeping the right bend. The rider's right leg rides the horse forward and controls its hind quarters. With its right eye, the horse sees traffic coming from behind and is able to make a clear passage for it to pass.*

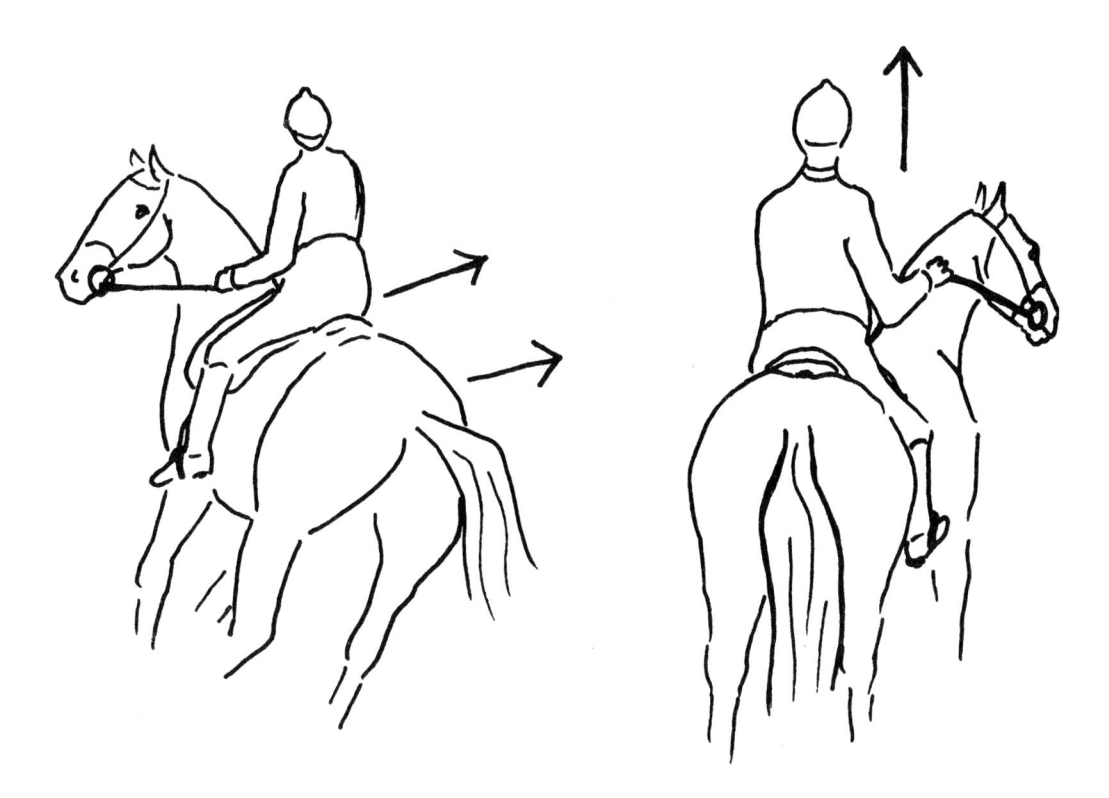

because it is frightened of something behind it than it is to stop a horse whipping round when it is frightened of something in front of it.

The method of moving a horse over to the left when looking right can also be used to keep horses out on the track and stop them "falling in" in serpentines and circles during a lesson.

Shying

Practise shying control during home lessons in a riding school or at Pony Club/riding club rallies.

Set up a "spook" such as a pile of sacks or some plastic bags at the B or E marker.

Explain to the ride that when a horse shies it looks at the spook and moves sideways (or sideways and forwards away from it) with its outside shoulder bulging and leading the way.

When a horse shies at something on the left most riders instinctively use their left rein. This is *wrong* because:
1. The horse then thinks the rider wants them to go even closer to this dangerous "spook" so they shy even more.
2. It is the right shoulder, which is leading the way, which needs controlling to prevent the horse shooting sideways so much.

If on approaching a spook on the left the rider notices the horse raise its head, prick its ears and shorten its stride that is the first "message" that it may shy. If riders were more observant and noticed the early warning signals of head carriage, ears and stride they would not so often be taken by surprise and perhaps "unshipped" by a sudden whip round from the horse.

Explain this and teach your ride to recognise signs given by their horse's head and ears.

As soon as the rider realises that their horse may shy at something on its left they must sit down on their two back seat bones and ride the horse strongly forward using their right rein to bend the horse's head away from the spook and using this right rein quite strongly to control the right shoulder and stop it bulging out. Their right hand can be lifted quite high

Lessons using barrels or cones   **133**

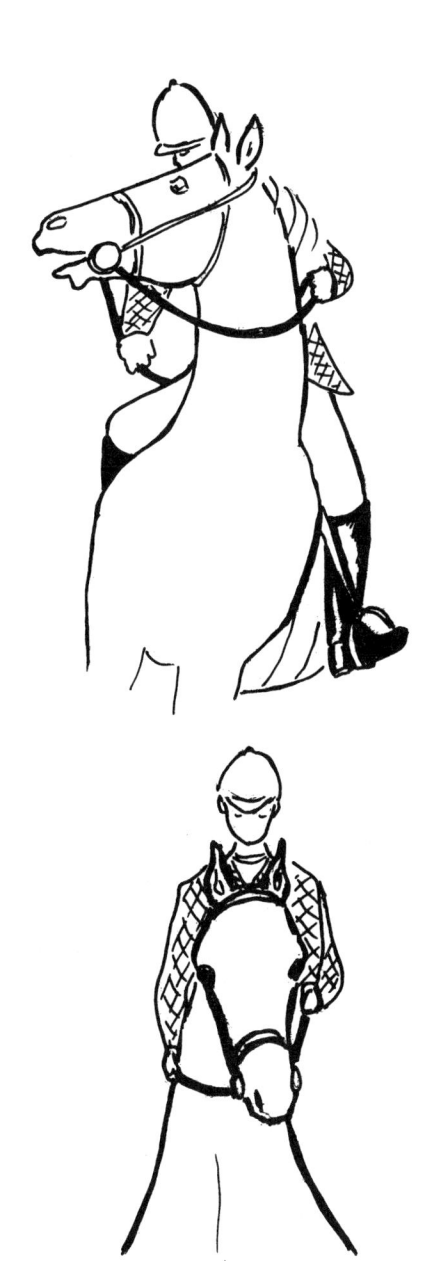

This rider (above, left) *is using the right rein only – the wrong way to control a horse which is shying out to the left. The horse goes sideways to the left, with its left shoulder leading. Shying* (above, right) *can result in the rider tipping forward, as here. This rider's stirrups are too long, his toes are down and subsequently when the horse shies he is nearly falling off. The correct way* (left) *to control a horse about to shy out to the left. The left rein is used to control the neck and left shoulder and the rider's left hand is raised for greater control of the neck. By using his right hand the rider is regulating the amount of bend in the horse's neck and by using his legs he drives the horse strongly forwards.*

for extra effect. Keep a contact on the left rein. Their right leg, used strongly, should control the horse's hind quarters and their left leg should keep it going forward. Their hands must allow their horse to go forward.

The priorities are:
1. To keep the horse going forward so do not ask it to pass very close to the spook.
2. To keep the horse looking to the right to control the right shoulder.

As soon as the horse's head is turned away from the spook it knows that the rider is not going to ask it to go up to it so it ceases to shy so violently.

Do not try to force the horse to keep a straight line as it passes the spook. It is better to keep going forward at an even pace and accept a slight curve in its track away from the spook. Whatever happens you want to avoid a "whip round" from the horse.

Practise spook control on both reins. For some reason (perhaps poor sight in one eye) some horses will pass an object first time in one direction yet shy violently at the same object when passing it for the second time when it is on their opposite side and seen with the other eye.

Also practise going up the centre line with a spook on the left before X and a spook on the right after X. This is a very important safety lesson because:
1. Horses shying at something on their left and having their heads bent to the left by the rider using the left rein, cannot see what is on their right. They are so intent on gazing at the spook (the rider is holding their head left, towards it) that they go sideways to the right, possibly into a ditch or barbed wire fence which they have not noticed. I have seen this happen several times. They can also shy out into the path of traffic.
2. When on a road, horses shying at something on their left and turned towards the spook by the rider's left rein, will move out into the road away from the spook and are likely to be hit by vehicles coming up behind them. Bent to the right, away from the spook, by the rider's right rein, the use of the rider's right leg ensures that their shy out into the road will be controlled and their right eye will see approaching traffic. This is a very important safety lesson.
3. Tell riders that if they are approaching something on the left that their

horse is likely to shy at, they should wait and pass it when there is no traffic going by.

Kicking

Kicking is not such a danger in riding schools where the horses probably know each other. Even here, though, some horses are jealous kickers and you must always be aware of them. A new horse introduced to a ride where all the other horses know each other must be drawn to the attention of the ride and constant warnings given to keep distances correct.

In an unknown ride, for instance at a Pony Club or riding club rally, you really have got to be very careful. Warn the ride constantly and where necessary quite severely for their own safety. You might give them a question and answer session:
Q. "What happens to you if you break your leg?
A. "You go to hospital and it is put in plaster until it mends."
Q. "What happens to a pony if another pony kicks it and breaks its leg?"
A. "A pony's leg cannot be mended and it has to be shot."
Q. "You don't want your pony to get a broken leg do you?"
A. "No."

So, don't get too close to the pony in front.

A little talk on these lines may seem brutal but it really is for the riders' own safety and it does make them think.

Put a kicking pony at the back of the ride and always be aware of its position and warn its rider and other children. In lines where it must be well out of kicking distance of others and in any group holding ponies during a lesson, be aware of the kicker's position. See that it is always a safe distance from others. If the pony is the sort that rushes backwards kicking out with both heels, ask someone to remove it (without upsetting the rider) and see if it can be taught separately. You cannot afford to risk the safety of the other animals or riders.

Teach all riders how to control a kicker. If their horse threatens to kick its neighbour on the right they will instinctively use their left rein to turn its head away. In doing this, however, they allow their horse to move its

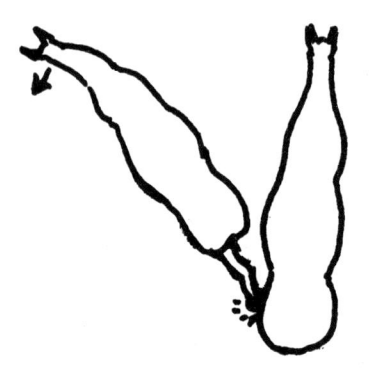

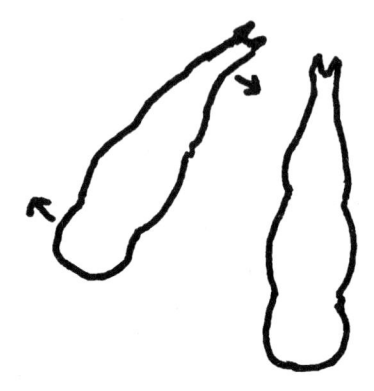

If a horse's head is (left) *turned* away *from its neighbour which it is trying to kick, it puts it into the best possible position for it to kick! The movement* (right) *of turning the horse's head* towards *the neighbouring horse means that the kicker's body moves away, therefore lessening the chance of the kicker landing a blow. This movement has to be taught to riders because it is* contra *to their instinct.*

hind quarters to the right, thereby putting it in the best possible kicking position. To prevent a horse kicking its neighbour on the right, riders should be taught that they must first quickly use their right rein strongly to turn their horse's head towards the horse that it wants to kick. Together with their right leg used strongly this moves its hind quarters away from the other horse.

This can be practised in pairs up the centre line, one being the kicker the other about to be kicked. The kicker must be seen to move their horse's head towards their partner and their hind quarters away. Practise from both sides and change characters. This is an important safety lesson which, if remembered, may prevent accidents now and in years to come.

Out on a hack

Do not believe a new client who says that they are an experienced rider. It seems to be human nature to overstate riding ability. Discuss exactly what their experience is and judge for yourself from the words they use, from their clothes and from the way they handle their horse or pony, and how they mount, adjust their stirrups and check their girth. If they do not do these things automatically, or do them incorrectly, beware.

Before you take a new rider out, see them ride their horse in a small enclosed area at all the gaits to be used on the hack. See if they can ride turns and circles accurately. If you are not happy about their ability either suggest that they have a lesson first before going out on a hack, or take them for a very slow hack on a very quiet horse or pony on a one-to-one basis (taking a lead rein).

Realise that going out on a hack is more difficult and potentially more dangerous than giving a riding lesson. The ride will not be in a small enclosed area where the horses are usually calm and obedient and where pupils are being given constant commands and help from the instructor. They will be in wide open spaces, going uphill and downhill, sometimes over rough and muddy ground. The horses will be much keener and riders will be expected to guide and control their horses accurately.

When they go to a new stables where their previous riding history is unknown, people often overstate their experience and riding ability if they want to go out on a hack. "I have been riding for five years," can mean that the rider has ridden once a fortnight on a lesson in an indoor school or fenced-in riding area. This in no way prepares them for going out on a hack where horses are often stronger and keener. Horses may show that they have minds of their own out on a hack and if another horse comes up level at canter they may want to try to race each other.

Keep an eye on your riding party – no more than six people to one escort. Notice who is the weakest and/or most unfit rider. Lead the way yourself and ask the other riders to stay behind you. Keep looking back to see that all is well and notice if any have a tendency to come up level. Do not trot or canter downhill or towards home. A horse tends to accelerate downhill just as you do if you run downhill. A rider feels more unbalanced and unsafe going downhill. If possible canter uphill where the riders feel safer and the gradient slows the horses down. Every horse and pony has a natural homing instinct and will tend to hurry towards home and even suddenly veer towards a turning for home. Be aware of this and plan your ride accordingly. Avoid turning round to retrace your tracks so that at one moment the horses are facing away from home and the next towards it. Try to choose a circular route or at least ride a loop to avoid a direct turn in your tracks.

Trot long enough before canter to enable you to look back to see that all the horses are trotting quietly and in a steady rhythm and are not pulling or fighting for their heads. Only canter if they are all calm and steady at a trot. If the horses are always ridden at a steady trot first they are far less likely to shoot off in canter.

Before cantering tell the ride where you intend to canter to, where you intend to trot again and where you intend to walk, so that if someone does pass you they know what your plans are. The danger is that if someone does pass you they become the leader and the other horses are very likely to follow them. It is a good idea to have the rule, "If anyone passes me everyone stops and stands still." It may not actually work but the riders will at least know what they should be trying to do.

Before you change gait, pace or direction or start to go uphill or downhill always look back and make sure there is no more than one horse's length between each horse. If there is a gap between horses or anyone is even slightly left behind slow down or stop to allow them to catch up before you proceed. A horse left behind may go faster and trot or canter to catch up and, especially downhill, may set the others off.

Remember that a frightened or tired rider may be very reluctant to admit to this situation. Ask frequently if everyone is all right. Before cantering ask if there is anyone who would rather trot instead. Somehow it is easier to say, "Yes," to this than to say, "No, I don't want to canter," in reply. If anyone expresses any doubts respect their wishes and go more slowly. Really listen in case a shy person speaks very quietly. If necessary put someone on a leading rein which you should always carry, just in case, or slow the whole ride down. Choose easy terrain, lanes and narrow tracks rather than wide open spaces and big fields which excite some animals and make the ride more difficult to control. In extreme cases it may be necessary to take the whole ride home at walk.

Riding is a high risk sport and all riders should be aware of this. If you think ahead, foresee possible problems and plan your route and terrain to suit the weakest rider in your group you should be able to conduct a hack safely. Never take unnecessary risks. When in doubt don't.

12 Trotting poles

One of the difficulties of using trotting poles in a ride can be horses or ponies of different sizes and different lengths of stride. There are two possibilities:
1. Two sets of poles at different distances side by side. Always start with one pole unless you know the horses and riders really well. Walk, then trot, over it in both directions and note the reactions of horses and riders who are new to you. The horse's expression – its face, eyes and ears – and the rider's position will tell you a lot.
2. Trotting poles placed in a fan shape. (For beginners or novice riders place a cone at each end of every pole.) Start with one pole, then use just the two outside ones before putting in the third central pole.

Approximate distances apart for trotting poles, should be:
Small ponies	1.10–1.30m (3.5–4.5ft)
14.2hh and short striding cobs	1.30–1.40m (4.5–4.75ft)
Larger animals or those with a naturally long stride	1.35–1.50m (4.5–5ft)

Do not ask the ride to walk their horses over poles set at trotting distance. The strides are wrong for walk and will confuse both horse and rider.

After one pole progress to two poles, double distance apart. (This will prevent animals jumping two poles set at the normal distance apart – something many often try to do.)

You have now got the first and third pole in place. When the ride have trotted in both directions over these two poles put a third pole in the gap between them.

Position the ride where they can see clearly, standing them to one side of the poles. They can then watch the approaching horse and see where its feet land in the gaps between the poles, noticing which are correct.

A hind foot should land exactly in the centre of the gap between the first two poles. If it is in the same central position in the gap between the second and third poles the distances are correct for that horse.

If the hind footmark is central in the first gap but further forward, nearly touching the third pole, in the second gap the distance is too short for that horse. If a horse knocks a pole and displaces it slightly, immediately re-position it correctly.

Fourth and fifth poles can be added gradually. Horses must go through trotting poles at an active trot. If they are allowed to slop along slowly and lazily they will take shorter strides and make the distances appear wrong, so make sure they look and feel as if they are "going somewhere".

Because you want horses working over trotting poles to round their backs and lower their heads and necks, work the riders in rising trot. If the riders sit to the trot some horses may go hollow, with their heads in the air. This is especially likely if a rider is not good at sitting trot and bumps about on the horse's back, leading to unsteady hands which jiggle and jolt the bit in the horse's mouth.

Start with one trotting pole (left) and then add two more as here. Horses are less likely to attempt to jump trotting poles laid out on the ground like this. The correct distance (right), the hoof marks have been imprinted by the horse centrally in both gaps.

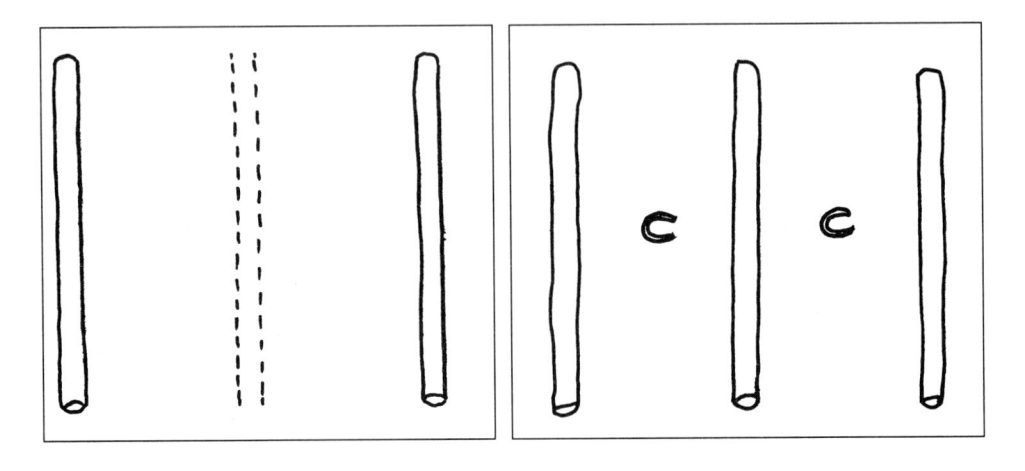

Trotting poles

Plan your trotting poles (or jumps) so that the outside track is always kept clear. If a horse is misbehaving, tearing along too fast, or if the rider is nearly falling off, the hazard of trotting poles or a jump will not then be in their path.

Do not let the ride follow on over trotting poles. If there is a problem or a fall it could be dangerous. Call the riders by name out onto the inside track to go over the poles. Give them plenty of warning so that they can prepare their horse.

By altering all the poles to be 15cm (6in) wider or closer you can help riders learn how to lengthen or shorten their horse's stride.

The ride can learn a lot by being in a position where they can watch the way of going and the foot falls of each horse. If something goes wrong ask them why and what to do about it. Try out their suggestions. If you keep their interest and get them to watch other horses and riders and really think they will learn so much more whatever they are doing.

Check the distances if a pole is knocked. Always make sure straight poles are parallel and distances are kept correct. Poles set at trotting dis-

Here (left) *the distance between the trotting poles is too long. The hoof mark is imprinted centrally in the first gap but is only just beyond the pole in the second gap. And here* (right) *the distance is too short. The hoof mark is imprinted centrally in the first gap but is way beyond the centre of the second gap.*

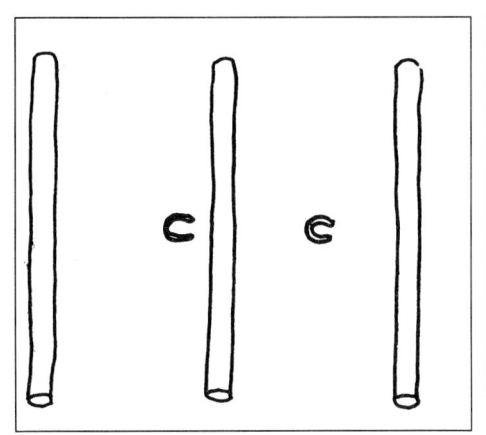

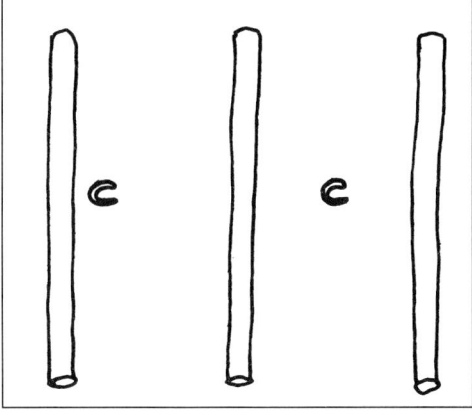

tance are not the correct length for walk so do not ask the horses to go over them at walk. The horses will hit them, become muddled and perhaps upset.

Fan shape

A boon to anyone taking a ride of mixed sizes and abilities is to use the trotting poles in a fan shape pattern.

Plan your fan on a corner on an inside track. You will need a cone or barrel to mark the point at the inside of the fan and a cone at the outside end of each pole.

Unless you have already just used the straight poles start with one pole. Try to use striped poles of identical colours. Place them so that horses travelling on a track exactly the same distance from the centre of the fan will be going over sections of the poles that are of the same colour.

Horses which are used to ordinary parallel trotting poles easily accept a fan. Horses completely new to trotting poles may find it puzzling at first.

Riders really do have to think, concentrate and ride their horses with

Coloured trotting poles in a fan shape. The markers at each end are to help keep horses and riders on the correct track.

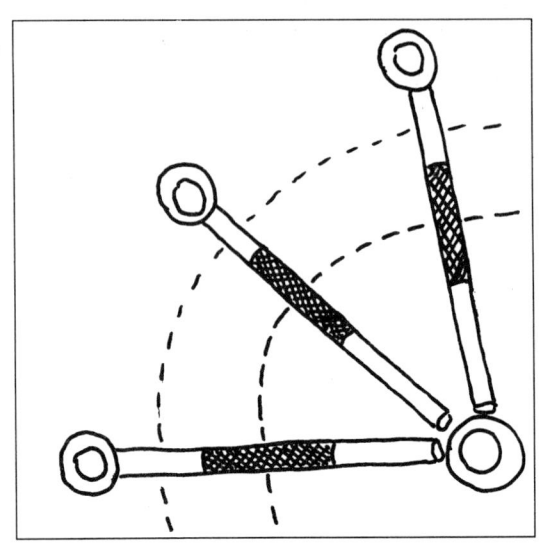

accuracy so that they go over sections of the same colour and therefore gaps of the same size.

The inside edges of the poles can be 45cm (18in) apart and the outside edges 1.5–1.7m (5–5.5ft) apart, each with a marker at the end. If you stand facing inwards towards the narrow "V", astride the centre of the three poles and about 1.5m from the "V" the ride can walk over the poles in front of you. Some 45cm apart is about right for ponies, 60cm (24in) for horses at walk. Next, work in rising trot and position yourself standing astride the centre pole this time facing outwards. With you in this position the ride must trot round you, trying to guide their horses exactly over the centre of each coloured strip on all the poles so that the distances between the poles they are stepping over are exactly the same.

If a big long striding horse is coming next can you move out towards the end of the poles where the gap between them is wider. If a small pony is coming you can move in towards the "V" so that where the pony will go round you the gaps will be narrower and will suit its stride.

Lengthening and shortening the stride can be practised without moving the poles.

The riders really do have to work and think and ride as if they are riding a small circle or they will be correct over the first pole but then drift further out and just make the second; then, having drifted even further out, they will face a long gap which their horse cannot possibly make to the third pole.

Working with fan-shaped poles is interesting for horses, for riders and for you. It is not suitable for beginners who are unused to trotting poles.

13 Jumping

Holding the mane

Many people disapprove of teaching beginners to hold the mane when learning to jump. My feelings are that if it works better than a neckstrap (and in my opinion it does) do it.

My reasons for telling pupils to hold the mane are:
1. They feel safer because it does not slip about as a neckstrap does.
2. By putting two elastic banded plaits in the place in the mane that they should hold you can control their body position. They will always hold the same place and so will bring their bodies forward the right amount. They will begin to get the consistent "feel" of being in balance and "going with" their ponies or horses.
3. If holding the mane saves a rider from falling off (which it often does) it must be a good idea.

The carefully chosen position of two elastic banded plaits helps to put the rider in the correct balanced position to jump safely. Here the rider's slightly rounded back will be improved as he gains in confidence.

4. The horse never gets a jab in the mouth if its rider holds the mane with both hands when jumping. This must be better for the horse.

The disadvantages of telling pupils to hold the mane are:
1. The rider's hands are fixed in one position.
2. They do not learn to "push their hands forwards towards the horse's mouth". However, I do not think beginners can cope with doing this

Jumping positions. A rather insecure position (above, left); the stirrup is too long, the rider's back is rounded and he is too far in front of the movement. An equally insecure position (above, right); the hands are too far forward, the lower leg is too far back, and the stirrup is too long, resulting in the rider being pulled forward and out of the saddle. The best position (left); the stirrup is shorter, the rider sits in balance with a flat back, goes with his pony, feels safe and secure and gains confidence quickly.

and with staying on board which must surely be the priority with anyone learning to jump.
3. Riders who learn to jump by holding on to the mane do tend to go on doing so when they should be learning to manage without it.

Holding a neckstrap

If a horse is hogged or has a very thin mane its rider will have to hold some form of neckstrap. Never teach jumping without something for your pupils to hold on to. Even top riders like to feel that they have got something to catch hold of in an emergency.

The disadvantage of holding on to a neckstrap is that it can slip about, forward or back and most disconcertingly sideways. If both of a rider's hands slip sideways down the same side of a horse's neck, as they can with a neckstrap, the rider is likely to fall off. With a neckstrap the rider's hand position can be anywhere from just in front of the withers to up near the horse's ears, so there is no consistent guide for their hand and therefore for their body position.

A leather breastplate which has two small straps coming from the top of its neckstrap, attaching to "Ds" on each side of the front of the saddle, does stay in place better if used as a rider's "handle".

Unless a neckstrap is adjustable and can be tightened so that it fits snugly much further forward than it would usually be worn, it does not help a rider to reach forward far enough and so move their body forward. Worn in the normal position, just in front of the withers, the small straps which stabilise it stop the rider's hands going forward as they should when jumping.

When pupils are safe and happy holding their two "handles" (the plaits in the mane) they should be encouraged to progress to holding a neckstrap and pushing their hands forward towards the horse's mouth to allow it to stretch its neck and head out freely when jumping.

A sad sight at many shows are those horses and ponies which are, or have been, jumped by riders who either jab them in the mouth when they do jump or who keep them in a very tight hold on a short rein in the approach and do not give them any more rein when they jump.

Such animals either throw their heads up in a desperate effort to avoid a jab in the mouth (and then jump hollow backed and with head in the air) or, although they want to jump, panic at the last minute. They refuse because they know that if they jump they will get a painful jab in the mouth or will be held so tightly (not being allowed to use their heads and necks) that they can't jump at all. They are then often beaten up for refusing. Often, too, these unfortunate animals are being ridden in a severe bit and perhaps a very tight martingale as well.

Teaching beginners to jump

I do not think that beginners should be taught to jump until they can guide and control a pony properly in sitting trot and can sit to the trot comfortably and correctly. As jumping often requires a larger and longer canter stride it is surely also common sense to say that before being taught to jump pupils should be comfortable and confident in canter sitting forward with shorter stirrups. They should be able to canter confidently with their seats up out of the saddle. They should also be able to trot in this position.

This is the position they are going to have to be in to go over a jump in comfort and without losing confidence. Small children and adults are so

A light forward seat in canter. The stirrup is shorter so the rider is better balanced and more secure in the saddle.

148   Teaching Riding

very often expected to learn to jump before their riding has got to this stage. Do not ask too much too soon. Loss of confidence and/or falls will occur.

If a rider approaches the jump with their seat in the saddle, as the animal's hind quarters come up, the back of the saddle hits their seat and throws them forward with an alarming lurch or tips them right off. On the next approach to a jump the now frightened rider, in apprehension, either sits upright not daring to lean forward as told, or braces their feet forward against the stirrups and sits back as if to delay the frightening moment when the animal jumps. In either of these positions the rider is even more likely to get thrown forward or fall off than on their first approach. This is disastrous. The pupil is really frightened and has quite understandably been completely put off jumping – probably for a very long time.

This situation with beginners jumping (child or adult) occurs far too often and is quite unnecessary. To improve matters:

1. Wait until the riders can ride at canter comfortably and safely.

Light contact on a horse's mouth and a suitable approach position on a horse that the rider knows will go first time.

2. Teach them to ride with a shorter stirrup, sitting forward with their seats out of the saddle at trot and canter.
3. If you want them to stay on board teach them how to hold the mane with both hands well before the jump. (A neckstrap is not so stable and can slip forward or sideways.)
4. Build jumps with really good wings so that no horse or pony will try to run out.
5. Start by sending the riders, in jumping position, through jump stands without even a pole on the ground so that all the horses and ponies will go forward confidently.
6. Progress to a pole on the ground, then tiny cross-poles so that the animals will go straight to the centre of the jump.
7. Teach your pupils to go forward with their mounts, seats up in the air out of the saddle, hands forward holding the mane (so that their upper bodies follow their hands forward and their seats are also lifted forward and up out of the saddle).

The rider must still, as on the flat, be in balance over their feet so they will find a saddle that is high in front and slopes down at the back more difficult to get forward in and keep the lower leg back.

I fully realise that there will already be mutterings from some readers that this is *not* how jumping *should* be taught. No, if we go by many books on the subject and stick to "purist" teaching riders should be taught to sit in the saddle in the approach and swing forward from the hips as the horse or pony takes off! As novice riders have no idea *when* the horse or pony is going to take off and will find moving their upper body considerably when the animal is just approaching the take off point a very difficult thing to do, I think it is not a reasonable, effective and confidence building way of teaching a beginner to jump whether it be a child or adult.

One or two plaits with elastic bands can be put in the pony's mane high enough up the neck to get the rider's upper body forward and their seat out of the saddle when holding on to them (but not so far forward that the rider is lying along the pony's neck with their lower leg going back). Marking the place to hold the mane helps to keep the rider's body consistently positioned and balanced in the approach. Just saying, "Hold the mane," is a very hit and miss affair. Too close to the front of the saddle and they are not forward enough so their seat does not have to come out of the saddle. For this reason telling them to hold on to the front of the saddle is not a good idea either because they can do this and still sit down in the saddle or even lean back so they will still be jolted in their seat by the back of the saddle as they take off. Holding the front of the saddle prevents their upper body coming forward correctly.

If they happen to choose a place in the mane to hold that is too far forward they are likely to be lying along the animal's neck with their lower leg going back. It is therefore better to mark the best place to hold with plaits.

This method of teaching beginners works for child or adult. They feel safer and gain confidence more quickly. Even after the first few attempts they still want to jump, and wanting to jump is what makes a rider go forward with their mount in the approach. The rider who *wants* to jump is more likely to keep their mount jumping happily too.

A few uncomfortable lurches and bumps from the back of the saddle

A good landing position. The rider is in balance with the horse and is also looking ahead to the next fence.

A bad jumping position. The rider is insecure and in front of the movement. He is leaning on his hands and his lower leg is too far back.

and perhaps a fall and they soon do *not* want to jump. Very probably as a result of this they begin sitting back in the approach to avoid the feared moment of take off. This is a vicious circle producing an even more uncomfortable experience over the jump. Their mount will be unhappy too!

People should not *have* to fall off when learning to jump. Using the method that I advocate, there should be very few falls.

The animals used for teaching jumping must be quiet and steady. They must go forward willingly and not refuse or try to run out. An animal which goes fast into a jump is only suitable for an experienced rider. The running out or refusing can be eliminated by working between jump stands with nothing on the ground and then progressing to poles and cross-poles. Building up very gradually like this there is no reason why animals should stop or run out. Wings or poles as wings are an asset when teaching beginners to jump. They must not be expected to control their mount; just thinking about their position is hard enough for them when learning to jump.

Holding the mane means that the riders cannot jab their mounts in the mouth by hanging on to the reins – a common cause of animals refusing.

Only when your pupils are confident, "going well", loving jumping and securely "going with" their ponies over the jumps should you progress further in their education. Then you can cease to give the previous, very simple instruction, "Hold the mane and stick your bottom up in the air", get their seats a little closer to the saddle, get them to feel and think about when the pony will take off and eventually approach a jump sitting in the saddle and swing forward from their hips at take off.

Guiding and controlling

This plan can be ridden in many different ways and used by all your pupils, from semi-beginners at walk with nothing between the pairs of markers to advanced riders with a variety of jumps between the markers.

Cones suitably placed train beginners to ride a smooth flowing course and get the "feel" of doing this correctly. As your riders progress you can ask them to "feel" and "think" where their horse had the wrong bend or were unbalanced and tell you about it after they have ridden the course.

It is an excellent exercise within which to practise half-halts.

To ride this exercise smoothly and flowingly it is necessary for the rider to learn to:
1. Guide and control the horse accurately.
2. Use half-halts.
3. Re-balance the horse and feel when it is unbalanced.
4. Get the correct inward bend, straighten the horse and change the bend.
5. Ride the horse forward.
6. Change their weight to indicate change of direction both without and with jumps.
7. Memorise a course.

A course of jumps for novice riders

Build a low inviting course which flows through easy changes of direction. Spreads can produce a very big jump if a horse or pony meets one on a long stride and stands off, so don't make wide jumps for learners.

If teaching in a riding school you will probably know your animals; which one doesn't like the wall jump for instance, so you can deal with that one individually.

Jumping   153

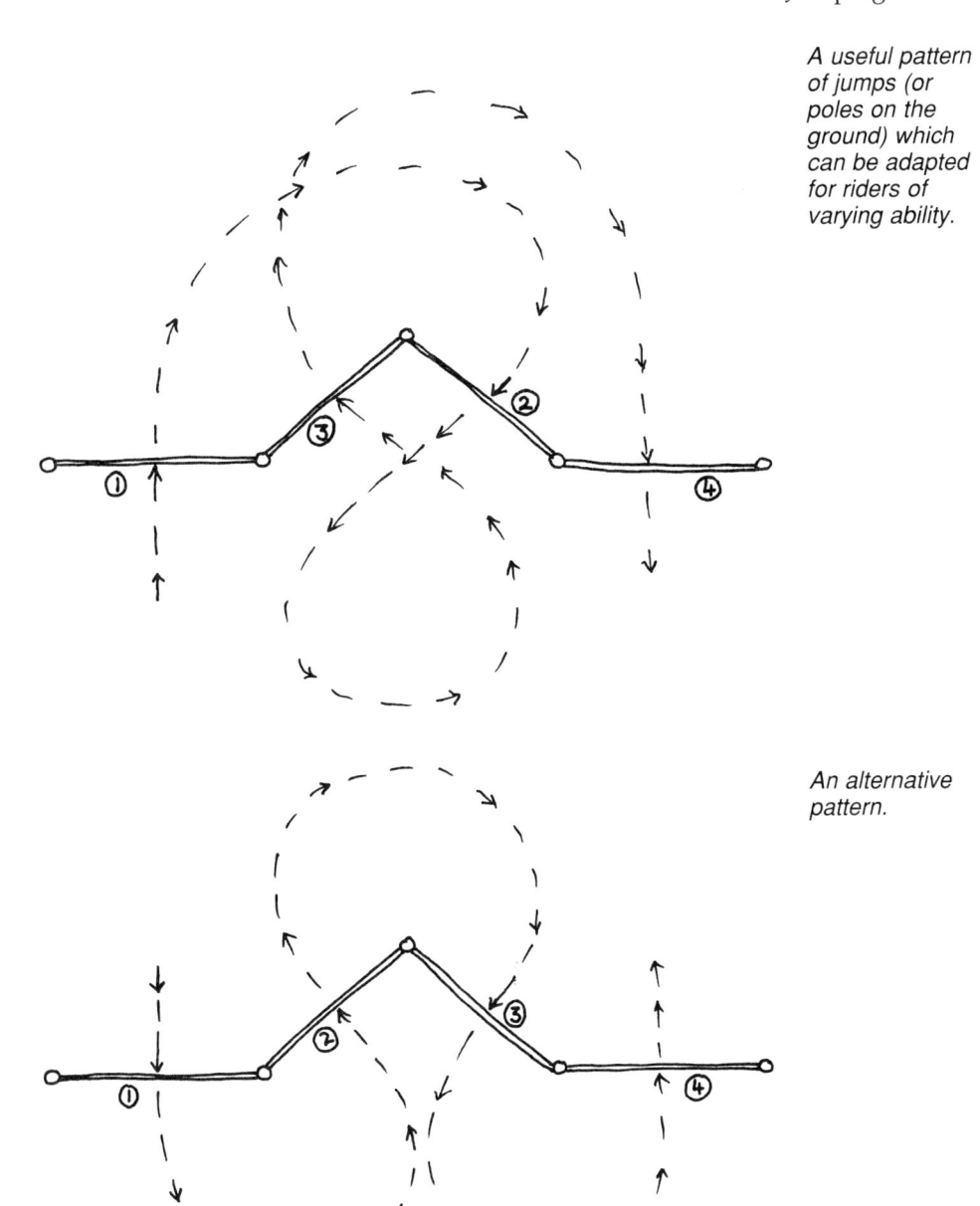

A useful pattern of jumps (or poles on the ground) which can be adapted for riders of varying ability.

An alternative pattern.

To introduce walls, brush fences, and so on to pupils learning to jump, and to young horses, open them up and let rider and horse go through the gap first.

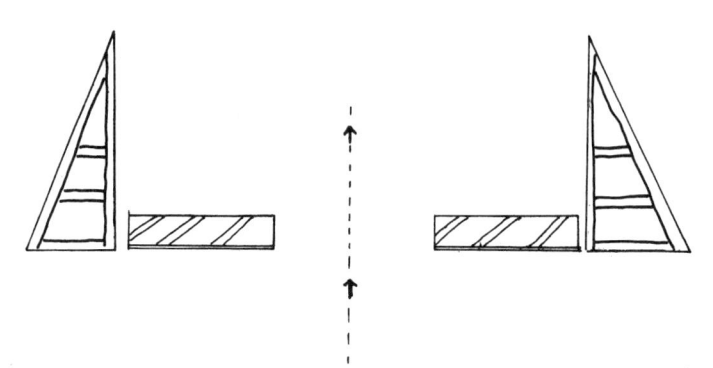

If you are teaching at a rally or a camp you may not know any of the animals but you should have learnt a lot about them by working up via trotting poles.

Teach with the thought that if there is a refusal it is your fault.
1. You have progressed too quickly.
2. You have not explained sufficiently.
3. You have asked too much of the horse.
4. You have asked too much of the rider.
5. You have built the jumps too narrow for the rider's ability.
6. You have made the jumps too "spooky" for the horse.

Start by taking one jump at a time. Place a simple, low cross bar as the first jump and, having asked them all to jump this in turn to get them going, proceed to jumps which can be opened up into two halves – bush fences, walls, straw bales and some types of filler for instance. Open them up so that there is a gap between the two halves approximately 2m (6.5ft) wide with just a pole on the ground in the gap. Let the ride walk then trot through the gap. Note which animals spook and shoot through the gap and get them to go again until they are confident and steady. Gradually close the gap and put a pole in it where necessary. (Make sure the pole is on the landing side of the jump so that it will easily fall down if hit.)

The double

When all the horses are happily negotiating jumps of this type in their normal position with the sections closed up together go to the next type of jump which causes trouble – the double.

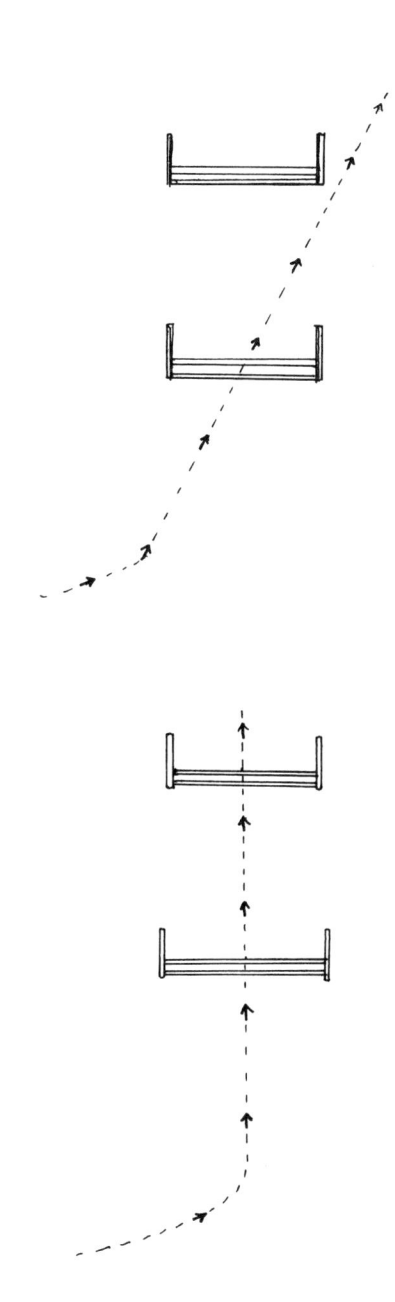

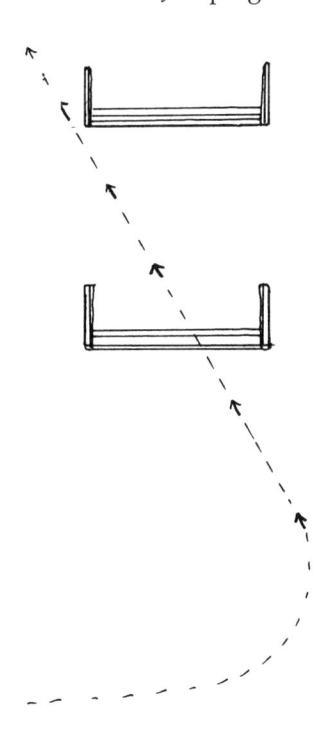

Jumping a double. Turning too soon (above, left) *the horse sees a gap to the right and is likely to run out.* Turning too late (above, right) *the horse sees a gap to the left and is likely to run out. The correct approach* (left), *the centre of the first fence in line with the centre of the second fence.*

Approximate distances apart should be:
- Ponies — 5.5–6.4m (18–21ft).
- Larger ponies — 6.4–7.0m (21–23ft).
- Horses — 7.0–7.4m (23–24.5ft).

Running out at the second part of a double is very common. Most often it is the rider's off centre approach which causes the problem. Position your ride so that they can see that if they turn into the double too soon the centre of the first part of the double will be in line with the gap to one side of the second half. The horse's eye will naturally be drawn to the gap that is straight ahead of it; therefore, the horse will be likely to aim for this gap and run out.

Likewise, if they go too far over in their approach and turn into the double too late the centre of the first part is now in line with the gap on the other side of the second fence. The horse's eye will naturally be drawn to this gap and it is now likely to run out there.

When riders are approaching the double tell them to plan the track they will ride very carefully. They must look at the track they are now on then look across to the two parts of the double and turn in when they can see that the centre of the first part of the double is exactly in line with the centre of the second part of the double. Their horse's eye will then be on the centre of both jumps and it is more likely to jump both.

Why does the second part of a double so often cause more trouble than the first part?

1. In approaching a double the horse may be thinking about and looking at the second half, perhaps wondering whether it likes the look of the straw bale under it for instance and it is still thinking about the second half when suddenly the first half is right there in front of it and it has not got time to get organised and jump – so it stops.
2. The horse and rider are in a bit of a dream lolloping along having successfully jumped two or three single jumps. The horse lollops over the first part of the double and is completely taken by surprise to find another jump so close. Its mind is not working very quickly so it lurches to a halt. This type of refusal is largely the rider's fault. They have not made sure that the horse was alert and thinking. They have

not told it, by half-halts, riding it forward into more contact, shortening it up and moving its centre of gravity further back that something different is going to happen. Preparation is necessary for the extra effort needed to negotiate two jumps close together.
3. The second part of the double is spooky. The rider rides into the first part then just sits, doing nothing with their legs, just hoping that the horse will go – but it doesn't, it stops.

If a horse lacks confidence the rider's feel on the reins, body weight and use of legs must all say to the horse, "Go on, it is perfectly all right. You are going to jump. I want to go."

If in the approach to a jump a horse feels that the rider's rein contact, body weight and lack of leg use are all saying either, "I am frightened of jumping," or "I don't really mind whether you jump or not," the horse is likely to stop at anything slightly difficult or anything slightly spooky even if it is just a rather idle horse and not really worried at all.

A young or nervous horse receiving the message that the rider is also nervous or uncertain thinks, "Well if you are frightened of it also it must be dangerous so I had better not jump." To partner a young horse or unconfident horse with a rider also lacking confidence cannot be good for either of them.

The easiest way to build up to jumping a double is to practise jumping just the second half first and making it really low. Come in from a circle so that the centre of the second part of the jump comes on the track of your circle and go away on the same circle. Repeat your circle approach on the other rein and only then approach the double in the normal way with the centre of both jumps in line. Using this method you will rarely get refusals because the horse will already know about the second half.

This is a good time to give lessons on knowing which leg a horse is leading with and on knowing which leg it has landed on. This work can be done when planning and riding changes of direction during the course.

To wake the horse up and gets its attention ready for jumping it is ridden forward in a preparatory circle into a holding hand; this shortens it up and moves its centre of gravity further back ready for jumping. If the first jump is on the left rein, the rider's preparatory circle should also be

To give a horse confidence, jump just the second fence before jumping both fences of the double together.

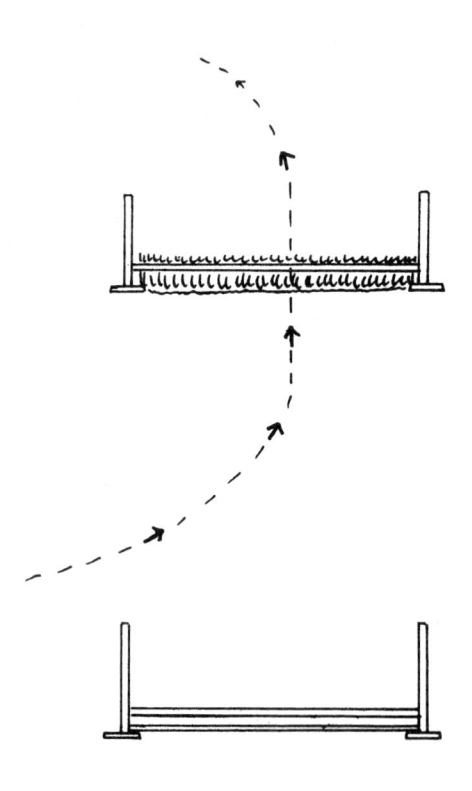

on the left rein in canter with the near foreleg leading. The rider's weight should be a little more into their left stirrup.

If there is a change of direction to the right after the second jump the rider must smoothly change more weight into their right stirrup and at take off look right, think right, ride right using the aids for canter with the off fore leading. The horse, feeling the rider's change of weight and the canter aids, should now change leg in the air and land with the off fore leading so that it is balanced, ready for the right turn. If it does so the rider can proceed in canter. If it lands still leading on its near fore it must be brought to trot (sitting) and immediately asked for the off fore lead.

If there is a change of direction after a double the change of the rider's weight should come at the second part of the jump. If at any time during the course the horse goes disunited in canter the rider should ride forward to trot and immediately apply the correct canter aids.

Between jumps the rider must use half-halts to re-balance the horse by riding forward into a slightly holding hand and keep it "short and bouncy" ready for the next jump. Ridden in this way the horse should be able to stay balanced and should jump in a good round shape.

If the horse is ridden round on a slack rein and just urged forward by the rider's legs it is likely to get more and more on its forehand, unbalanced and heavy in front. It will jump long and flat, becoming more unbalanced as it lands after each jump. When the rider does want to steady or turn the horse he or she will find it difficult to do so.

Learning to ride a good track.

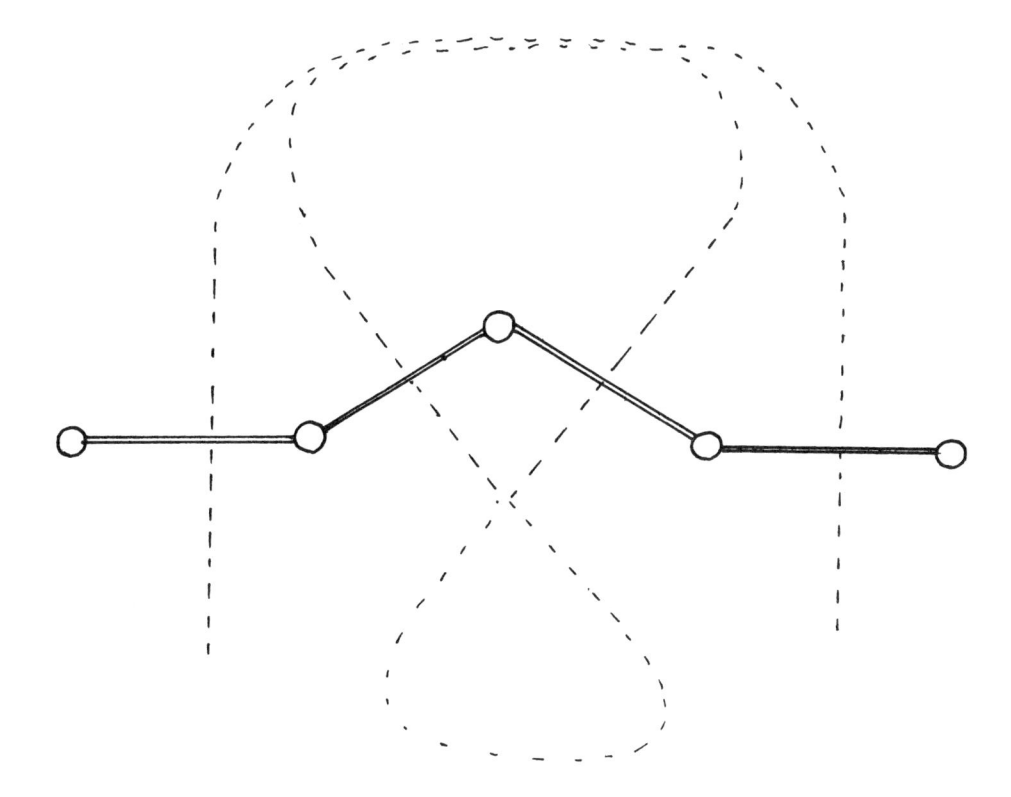

It is the way that the horse is ridden between fences and in the approach that produces a good round balanced jump or a flat unbalanced one.

Hopefully, by the time horse and rider are jumping against the clock, they will have learnt to produce the correct lead. Young horses should learn to jump a course in trot, rounding their backs and keeping a rhythm. Only then should they be asked to jump from canter. With young horses it is far better to take things slowly and get the correct balanced approach into a jump rather than have them unbalanced or disunited in canter.

Riders need to think and feel what is happening under them before they race round against the clock hauling unbalanced animals about by the reins as seen only too often at shows.

Horses that refuse

Why are they refusing? Perhaps the rider is frightened? Perhaps something is painful for the horse – its back, its feet landing on very hard ground? Perhaps it has had a fright at some time and never forgotten.

Having tried to find the reason, start with jump stands with nothing between them and progress to a pole, cross-poles and tiny fences of every type but always small enough for the horse to be kept facing the jump and made to climb over it somehow the first time it is put at it. It must be got

The wrong way to sit on a horse which does not want to go forward.

into the horse's head that it must get to the other side first time and there is no turning for a second attempt. Having been made to climb over, immediately ask the horse to jump the same fence again.

It is far better to get over a tiny jump first time than to get over a large jump at the third attempt.

Rushing fences

Why is this horse rushing at a jump? Is it because it is thinking, "Whoopee I love jumping,"? Or is it frightened that jumping will be painful so it is wanting to get it over quickly?

These are the two commonest reasons for a horse rushing at a jump.

In neither case are you going to do any good telling the rider to, "Hold it back more." Nor is a more severe bit going to be of any use. Neither of these suggestions really slow a horse down with lasting effect. The rider cannot slow a horse down by holding it back.

A plan and way of approach must be thought out so that the horse no longer wants to rush.

Turning in very short to a simple pole at walk can help. Next settle the horse through constant circles into a rhythm of rising trot. Never steady the horse or attempt to hold it back. Just turn in so short, barely one stride, that it drops its head and is over the pole. Go away on the same circle. Gradually increase the number of poles but always turn in so short that the horse has no opportunity to speed up before it gets to the poles, and always circle away in the same direction to continue the circle afterwards.

The rider must sit quietly in balance with the horse all the time. In the field have several sets of jump stands spread about with no poles between them. Ride in rising trot in continuous circles anywhere among the stands without going between them. Don't use the reins to steady the horse, use the circles. Only when the horse is trotting in a calm, steady rhythm should the rider start to ride between the uprights, going in and away on a circle. It does not matter if the rider or the horse gets a bit tired; keep the rising trot going and now put a single pole in between some of the jump stands. When the horse is negotiating this quietly make a small cross pole jump. If the horse gets at all excited, circle or go only through the stands without a pole or over just the single pole. In other words if the horse gets excited and hurries, go back a step. When the horse wants to walk let it and finish.

If this is done twice a day there should be a big improvement in the horse's attitude to jumping as long as the rider sits quietly in balance, never holds the horse back and never touches its mouth over a jump or pole.

As long as the horse does not try to hurry in trot go higher and vary the type of jump, but always have a pole on the ground between jump stands to revert to if necessary and stay in rising trot. Never jump two consecutive jumps. Always circle before and after each fence.

When the horse will stay in rhythm approaching, over and after landing from any fence, begin to try two consecutive jumps then circle after the second one. Introduce a couple of strides of canter before take off and circle to get trot again on landing.

This method really does work but needs constant repetition for the effect to last.

Young horses

Always ask your pupils the ages of their horses in a ride if they are unknown to you.

Young horses may tire more easily. They may never have been schooled in an indoor school or fenced-in area. They may never have been schooled within an area 40x20m in an open field. They may not be accustomed to being ridden with other horses so may get very excited or perhaps be nervous of the next horse behind them in the ride. They may never have seen trotting poles. They may never have jumped. Their rider may never have owned, ridden or schooled a young horse before. See my earlier book, *The ABC of Breaking and Schooling Horses*, for more help.

If something goes a little wrong with one horse in the ride and only then do you discover there is a problem when the rider says, "Well it's only a four year old, it's never been in a group of horses before," the mistake is yours. Give the young horse frequent rests with the rider off its back. Introduce it to things gradually. If you are changing horses in the ride don't put another rider on the young horse unless he or she is used to young horses and is a considerably better rider than the youngster's own rider.

Start the young horse's canter work with the rider sitting forward out of the saddle, stirrups a little shorter than usual. It will find it easier to round its back behind the saddle to break into canter and stay cantering with the rider's weight well forward off its back.

If it is absolutely terrified of even one trotting pole on the ground (and some are) put two poles in a line with a 2m (6.5ft) gap between them and let it follow another horse through the gap or follow you on your feet after you have spoken to it and rubbed its forehead. Gradually close the gap until it is going over a pole happily.

Always have jump stands or cones on each side of the poles for young horses so that they will not learn to run out. Build up to jumping very gradually making sure that the horse is always going forward confidently and willingly and is going straight for the centre of the jump. Build jumps which invite the horse to go straight to the lowest part in the centre. Have wings or good uprights to guide it in.

Make it easy, by good planning, for the horse to do what you want it to.

Teaching adults

Nearly all of the suggested exercises and amusing things to do in a children's ride are really enjoyed by adult riders too. Teaching them to ride can be fun. It does not have to be serious just because they are adults.

They also like "doing" things and knowing they have negotiated a handy horse course at walk successfully gives them a sense of achievement. Perhaps they will get confidence from seeing that they are not "the worst in the class" as they had previously thought.

By using the exercise with barrels and cones adults and everyone else in the ride know that if they have successfully guided and controlled their horse through them they have achieved something. When they go on to doing the, now familiar, exercises in trot they will have made progress. Everyone can see the progress they have made because they are all quite obviously much better than they were. Now no barrels are missed out or hit by riders' feet. There is a measure for their progress and the barrels and cones give turns and circles a purpose.

One word of warning: if you are quite young and used to mostly teaching children be careful not to "talk down" to a class of adults older than you. Treat them with respect.

14 Teaching can be fun

Teaching pupils to ride, be they children or adults, does not have to be deadly serious. In this chapter I have suggested some ways of lightening the teaching so that everybody can join in and have fun whilst at the same time learning.

Teaching boys

Some Pony Club rallies and camps have a Boys' Ride. This is a challenge for you as an instructor because boys' attitude to learning is quite different to that of girls. Boys mostly do not care whether they learn to ride nicely or correctly and they think grooming, especially tack cleaning, a complete waste of time. There is frequently a clown among them who is out for laughs, often at your expense.

Some boys can be quiet, timid, nervous people; others can be so foolhardy that you may find them doing something absolutely lethal to get attention from the rest of the ride. (Probably behind your back.)

They need to learn something challenging or something exciting through fun – or through bribery: "If you do this properly you can do cross-country afterwards."

For safety's sake you must have respect, control and obedience from boys but you must like them and they must enjoy your lessons. They need "a long rope", but they need, too, a good sharp pull on it when necessary.

Western riding is an obvious winner. Jumping off against the clock, with heavy penalties for roughness and bad style and being the show jumping hero of their choice is very popular.

Riding bareback is an excellent challenge but unfortunately is rarely done now, possibly because of the fear of it being considered too dangerous a thing to have been doing if a rider does have a fall and is injured.

Many years ago all pony clubs rode and jumped bareback regularly and the riders learnt a lot in the process. It was great fun and concentrated the mind, especially when jumping!

In those days no one was automatically sued if there was an accident.

Pony Club camp/rallies – the youngest ride

The youngest ride at camp or at a Pony Club rally is the most difficult ride to take. The only people who don't believe me will be the ones who have never taken this ride! To start with:

1. You are very limited as to what you can do to occupy them because of their age and inexperience.
2. Their attention span is very, very short.
3. Some ponies will refuse to budge in any direction.
4. Another will take off flat out, with screaming whinnies, to join big sister's pony in another ride.
5. One little mare will keep walking up to the other ponies and squealing and striking out at them.
6. One will stop dead every time it does a dropping and take a long time doing one!
7. One pony without grass reins will spend its whole time with its head down eating grass.
8. The pony with the grass reins will dive its head down so hard that it pulls its saddle forward in front of its withers, the girths are now behind the knees and its rider is slowly sliding head first down its neck towards its ears.
9. One pupil will want to go home.
10. And another will want to go to the loo.

Have I said enough to convince you?

If you do not have lots of experience with small children and little ponies it is not fair to the children or to you to take on this ride. I have seen so many keen, young instructors come in at lunch on the first day of camp shattered and disillusioned. They have had just one morning with the youngest ride and are wondering what on earth they can do to occupy their ride for the rest of the week and if they themselves will stay sane!

You really do need to like and understand small children and little ponies and to have had a lot of experience with both to take this ride at camp. You must use your imagination to keep their interest. They must all be doing something – not sitting in a dream ignoring your voice. Six riders (with two helpers) is more than enough for one instructor. Eight riders, even with four helpers, is a lot to cope with. Many things can only be done at walk.

You also need a very long and varied list of possible occupations for your ride. Make this a mix of mounted and dismounted activities because they may tire easily, especially if it is very hot. However long your list is you will invariably wish you had thought of more things to do and made an even longer list.

I have often heard it said, "Just occupy the smallest ride and keep them happy. You can't really teach them anything."! I do not agree with this at all. This is the most important ride of all because if they are allowed to sit all wrong and not have to do things properly and think what they are doing, and why, they will develop bad habits perhaps for life.

Make the words you use to praise and correct fun. "Look at Mary she is sitting up beautifully with a nice straight back." Hopefully one or two others will then sit up. To the child sitting in a round shouldered heap with a collapsed back, "Poor Henry, he looks as if he has got a pain in his tummy." Crouch forward, with your own back rounded, clutch your stomach and say, " 'Ow, 'ow." They laugh and hopefully Henry sits up. If he is still in a curved heap walk up behind him when he is at halt and say, "I have got a very sharp nail in my hand and if you don't sit up I will stick it into the middle of your bent back. It's coming nearer. Can you feel it?" (as you poke the middle of Henry's back with your finger). "Move your back forward out of the way quickly." This usually works and everyone enjoys it, including Henry.

You must be prepared to act, pretend and if necessary make a fool of yourself. A vivid imagination is essential when taking this ride. While they are walking round ask lots of questions to do with ponies, riding, saddlery. Make them easy, make sure everyone gets a turn. There is sure to be a "clever clogs" who knows every answer so give them a more difficult one to shut them up.

Where applicable don't just accept a correct answer, ask why? It makes the ride think and remember.

Teach about safety and danger

As we saw earlier, a question and answer session with pupils can teach them to think about dangers.

"What might happen if you get too close to the pony in front?"

"What might happen if you get on your pony before someone has tightened the girths for you?"

Even this ride, like those adults discussed earlier, should be taught to sit on their bottoms on their two back seat bones. A successful way of teaching this method is "Squash my hand".

Squash my hand

[*Warning*: This is a successful method but one which involves touching pupils' backsides. A tutor could get into hot water if his or her actions were misinterpreted so this method should be used with due caution.]

Get the ride to halt then go along the line asking each pupil in turn to stand up in their stirrups and lean forward out of the saddle. Put your hand flat on the saddle, palm down, just where their seat bones will come when they sit down. Now tell them to sit down and, "Squash my hand" At first you will not feel much happening but as you tell them to sit tall and lean back a little (and, to the round backed, "Stick your tummy out forward more") you will begin to feel their seat bones pressing into your hand.

That is the moment to say, " 'Ow, you are hurting my hand." Whereupon they probably do it even harder and more successfully so you say, "Stop, stop you are so good at it now I want to take my hand out." They really enjoy waiting for your shrieks of pain as you go down the line and you can now teach them to sit on their two back seat bones when riding by just saying, "Squash my hand," leading on to, "Squash my hand and use your legs," so that they learn to sit on their bottom and ride their ponies forward at the same time.

There is no reason why this ride should not sit as well as any other. They can and they will if you show them how, help and encourage them. Lots of, "Look Henry's pain in his tummy is better today, he can do 'Squash my hand' better than anybody now."

When they are sitting properly concentrate on getting their legs in the right place so that they are sitting in balance over their feet. Common faults are pushing against their stirrups and stiffening their knees as they do so. Some will be inclined to stand in their stirrups when they steady their ponies or to try to stop them by just pulling on the reins.

To make them think and remember not to push against their stirrups or stand up in them when using their reins pretend to cut their stirrup leathers nearly through where the stirrup iron hangs and tell them what you have done. (It must look quite convincing because once a child said to me, "My mummy will be very cross with you."!) Now say, "Don't lean on your stirrups or the stirrup leathers will break and the stirrup irons will fall onto the ground."

Backward sloping saddles will make it very difficult for them to sit correctly and keep their lower leg back so that they are sitting in balance over their feet. Well-built saddles to fit wide ponies and small riders are not easy to find. Ask them to sit further forward in their saddles and bend their knees. When they look down over their knees without bending forward they should not be able to see their toes. If they can see them say, "Hide your toes back further out of sight." The correction "Hide your toes," can then be used when lower legs come forward (as long as this has not happened because their seat has slipped back in the saddle).

To correct their foot position say, "Toes up, heel down." Use both sayings because one will work for this rider and the other for that one. "Heels down," often makes riders stiffen and brace against their stirrups so that their leg comes forward. "Toes up," can work better.

Another imaginary picture that works well is, "Your boots are full of water and you must not let any of the water fall out of that hole in the toe of your boot. If your toe goes down like this, all the water will run out." Demonstrate toe down with your own foot. "To keep the water in you must keep your toe up like this." Then as a correction, "Mary, the water is coming out of the toe of your boots."

Teach them sitting – not rising – trot and then they can continue to sit upright on their back two seat bones and keep the good position that you are trying to give them the feel of. They will feel safer because they are not wobbling about tipping forwards. They will feel safer because they are closer to the saddle. Many children wobble and lose their balance at the height of their rise in rising trot. If their pony puts its head down they will stay on better in sitting trot. They can hold the front of the saddle, lean back against their hand and if necessary be led in turn at sitting trot by helpers. Concentrate on position whatever the game you are playing. It matters all the time. Use sitting trot in all little games and competitions. You want them to begin to find it easier to use than rising trot when they want to get a pony to go forward, to guide it accurately round markers or when it argues.

How many children do you see still busily rising when they are trying to get their ponies to go forward or when they need to guide a pony accurately round a marker and it is being awkward? They are having problems because they have never learnt to use sitting trot as a more effective way of riding. They have never learnt to sit on their bottoms and ride their ponies forward on the track that they want them to take.

Sitting trot is just something they do for a few minutes during a lesson. They bounce about and slip sideways, so feel unsafe and hate sitting trot because they have never been taught how to sit, how to use the small of their backs and tummies coming forward, forward, forward in time to the trot so that they can sit to it.

Tell them to sit on their back two seat bones, think, "Lean back," and allow their tummies to come forward, forward, forward with the rhythm of the trot.

I know that it is a sweeping statement but I do think that sitting trot is very rarely properly taught. Pupils are not taught in detail how to sit and why. Sitting trot is not used nearly enough. Rising trot is the measure by which learner riders are judged. "Can you rise yet?" is the first question asked when someone starts to learn to ride. I would like it to be, "Can you do sitting trot comfortably yet?" Then, "Can you guide and control your horse/pony at sitting trot yet?" And only when pupils can do that should they be taught to rise by which time because they have got a good position, sitting in balance over their feet, rising should be easily learnt and usually is after such a good grounding.

Continue to use mostly sitting trot then let them do something like bending using rising trot, then sitting trot to do the identical exercise again. Ask them which way was easier to control their ponies, rising or sitting. They are likely to say sitting which will prove that you have taught them something. You are hoping to educate them so that as soon as they have a problem they automatically go into sitting trot to "boss" an awkward pony which doesn't want to obey their aids or to be ridden accurately.

Small children tend to use 95 per cent rein and only 5 per cent leg. I do not believe that this should be accepted. From the very beginning they must be taught that a bit in a pony's mouth hurts if they pull hard on the reins. They must say, "Please turn," when they use their reins. Practise them turning and actually saying, "Please turn," to their ponies as they do so. Because they are probably used to being told to be polite and say, "Please", it really does make them noticeably politer and more gentle with their reins. The correction then becomes, "Jane, you did not say 'Please' with your reins." The same applies to halt – no pulling on the reins only. Sit up tall, lean back a little, squeeze your pony's sides with your legs, lift your hands up a little and say, "Please halt" (or "Please stop") as you feel gently on the reins. Again to ask your pony to halt say, "Please."

Explain that you can thank ponies for being good by stroking their necks or by giving them a little rest.

If at the end of Pony Club camp your ride can sit on their bottoms and guide and control their ponies comfortably at sitting trot, using their legs and not hauling them about with their reins you will have done a good job and be proud of your ride. If you have enjoyed entering into their imaginative world and using it to teach and feel that they have enjoyed it too and learnt a lot, you will have done an excellent job.

Teaching but also amusing and interesting your ride

1. Rising trot or sitting trot saying the two-time words, Sun-day, Mon-day, Tues-day, Wens-day, Sun-day, etc.
2. Canter saying the three-time word Sat-ur-day, Sat-ur-day in time to canter.

3. Really difficult. Go from trot to canter saying Sun-day, Mon-day, etc., then onto Sat-ur-day, Sat-ur-day without missing a beat even when returning to trot and Sun-day, Mon-day again.
4. Rhythm rising. Sit, sit, sit, rise one beat, sit, sit, sit, rise one beat. Because it is an odd number of "sits" they stay on the same diagonal. An even number of "sits", say four, and they change diagonal. Some find it easy, some find it very difficult.
5. Sitting trot. They shut their eyes for a second then start rising immediately. They must very quickly say which diagonal they are on by "feel".
6. Lengthening and shortening the stride. Count how many strides of trot/canter their horse normally takes between the two quarter markers on the long side of the school (or between the two markers in any chosen open space). Then count how many small strides they can fit in before seeing how few long strides will fit in.
7. Chain. Divide your ride into two, going on opposite reins three lengths apart. The first pair meet and pass each other left shoulder to left shoulder, pass the next person right shoulder to right shoulder and so on bending in and out of the oncoming ride in a "chain". Practise at walk first.
8. Touching points of the horse or parts of saddlery while riding. Choose the gait to suit the ability of the ride. For instance you say, "Left stirrup iron, poll, cantle, point of shoulder." They have to know where everything is and learn to keep their balance in different positions while the horse is moving.
9. Transitions while the horse is moving. Done individually you will say one word of command and they must carry it out as smoothly but as quickly as possible. They must ride correctly – no massive kicks or heaving on the reins. For the inexperienced you would say, "Trot, walk, halt," and perhaps go from halt straight to trot. For the experienced, "Halt, canter, halt," is more demanding. The accent must be on smoothness not quickness.
10. Reins in one hand in a bridge. One rein comes in from the horse's mouth over the rider's little finger, across their palm and out between the thumb and index finger. The other rein comes in between their thumb and index finger, lies across their palm on top of the first rein

and out via their little finger. The reins are held with the hand flat, knuckles upwards. With both reins in the left hand, to turn left, carry the left hand knuckles upwards across to the right of the horse's withers so that there is slight pressure on the left side of the horse's mouth and almost none on the right side. Bend the wrist so that the left thumb goes towards the horse's head and the little finger comes towards the rider thus moving the bit on the left side of the horse's mouth to ask it to go left. To go right take the left hand across to the left, this time turning the wrist so that the little finger goes towards the horse's mouth and the thumb comes towards the rider and is used with the index finger to turn the horse. Practise serpentines and bending with the reins in one hand. Change hands.

11. Potato picking. Put two buckets one each at the B and E markers either up on barrels or tied to safe, steady jump stands at a height where riders can easily reach into them. Place a few more potatoes in each bucket than there are riders. Spread the ride out round the school. As they ride round with their reins in one hand they must take a potato out of the first bucket they come to and put it back into the next bucket. Change rein and change hands. The buckets can be placed on an inside or an outside track. If the buckets are on an inside track both reins must be in the outside hand to leave the inside hand free for "potato picking" and vice versa. More experienced riders can do this at trot. It can also be used for small children using both hands on the reins. To make it easier tie a knot in the reins at the correct length for control or they will keep dropping one rein as they fiddle with the potato. Warning: some ponies are frightened when the potato "plonks" into the bucket and may shoot sideways unshipping small riders. Practise being led first or at first "pretend" to pick up a potato and "pretend" to put it in the next bucket.

12. Western riding (neck reining). Hold both reins in one hand, coming into their hand from the horse's mouth between their thumb and index finger and leaving their hand by their little finger. Or both reins coming into their hand by their little finger and leaving between their thumb and their index finger. Say, "Carry your hand above the pommel of the saddle with your thumb on top. Western horses are trained to 'neck

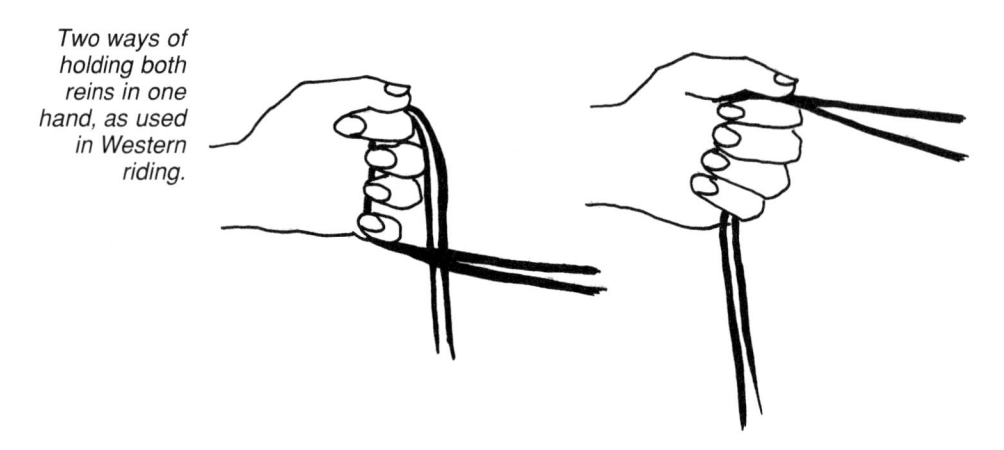

Two ways of holding both reins in one hand, as used in Western riding.

rein'. So to turn left carry your rein hand forward and left so that the right rein lies on the horse's neck halfway along it and presses on the right side of the neck. There should not be any pull on the right side of the mouth, just light contact. There should be no contact on the left side of the mouth." Western horses are trained to answer to the slightest change of the rider's weight and move in that direction, so smoothly move the weight a little back and over to the left. Look left, think left. To go to the right, move the weight to the right, the rein hand to the right, put rein pressure on the left side of the horse's neck, look right, think right. To go forward, move the rein hand forward, the weight forward and use the legs. To slow down or stop bring the weight back, legs smoothly on the horse's sides. Bring the rein hand up and towards the chest. Practise turns, circles, smaller circles, bending, stop, go. Let them get the feel of the smooth flowing swing of Western riding. It is surprising how quickly some horses and ponies understand and enjoy it too!

13. Scavenger hunt. You need a small bag for each child to put things in. The make a list of natural objects which may be found near the riding area – an oak leaf, a feather, a daisy, a dock leaf, an acorn, a piece of bark, a pebble, a snail, a worm (this can cause shrieks!). About ten objects are sufficient. For little ones no cantering is allowed or it can all get a bit wild. An older and younger child can go in a pair. Tiny riders

can be on the lead rein. Older riders have to get off and on again between each object collected.
14. Plait. Put your ride on an inside track two or more lengths apart. Leading files in succession turn inwards and pass on the inside of the first person they meet then on the outside of the next, "plaiting" their way through the ride. On passing the last person they circle from the outside track inwards and take their place two or more lengths behind the last person ready for the next rider coming. This exercise can be done at walk or trot but stay in walk until everyone gets it right and then go on the other rein. (Never work from rear to front as the riders will then be coming up behind each horse to pass it and their horse could get kicked.)
15. Cogs in a wheel. Put your ride in two circles on opposite reins. Put two markers 1.5m (5ft) apart on each side of the track at X where the two circles will converge. Spread the riders out three or more lengths apart. The riders go through the markers alternately, one from each circle. This can be done at walk, trot or canter according to the ability of the ride. Stay in walk until they have all got it right. Change the rein.
16. Pairs.
    a.   Round the school in pairs. The outside person has to work hard to keep up on corners, the inside person has to steady on corners so that they keep knee to knee.
    b.   Two riders on opposite reins. Start in pairs up the centre AC line. At the top one rider goes right and the other left. They must look across and stay level with their opposite pair so that they meet again accurately at the bottom of the centre line and ride up as a pair knee to knee.
17. Scissors. Two rides three lengths apart on opposite reins pass each other left shoulder to left shoulder. As they come to the first quarter marker on the long side both leaders change the rein diagonally across the school to the opposite quarter marker. They pass each other at X going alternately one from each ride. They always pass left shoulder to left shoulder when the two rides meet on the track. Having changed reins the ride which was on the inside will now be on the outside track. Always name the person who is to go across X first to avoid a collision.

18. Handy pony as a ride.
    a. Make a flowing course round and across the school which can be ridden on both reins – for example, cones to bend through, a narrow passageway of planks to go between, a pole on the ground, two straw bales to go between, a marker in a corner to go outside, two piles of sacks or something spooky to go between. Start at walk, individually and well spaced out so that if one rider has a problem there will not be a pile up, then progress to going as a ride at walk then trot. Riders can take it in turns to be leader.
    b. Teams – make two identical courses each using one long half of the school (perhaps include picking a coloured ribbon out of a bucket or putting a potato in a bucket). One rider goes from each team and when they finish they touch the next one in the team who can then start. Or make a finish line which the first one must cross before the next one starts.
19. Collecting ribbons. Cut as many different coloured pieces of material as there are riders (and one or two extra colours as spares) into five or six strips. Spread all the other pieces anywhere at riders' hand level (or low down if you want them to dismount and mount between each "find"). Give each rider one strip of material and tell them to find four more like it. It is safer to say, "No cantering," and warn them to look where they are going to avoid collisions.
20 Mr McGregor's Garden (from Peter Rabbit). For small children. The school is divided so that the garden occupies approximately two-thirds of the school which has cones and markers (the carrots and cabbages) to ride through and round. The smaller area, which must be big enough to hold all the ponies safely, is the "safe place". They ride about in the garden at walk until you say, "Mr McGregor is coming." The last one into the safe place is out (but have lots of practices first so everyone has a good go before being out). It is safer to say, "No cantering." A carrot is an appropriate prize for the winning pony!

The accent should be on teaching. Correct and explain your corrections. If there are problems discuss why they have happened and what to do about it.

It can all be good fun but the horses and ponies must enjoy it too and not be hauled about by the reins or ridden roughly in the excitement of the moment.

Real progress in riding and jumping can come from doing interesting things which make every horse and rider "think" and "ride" most of the time.

Teaching but also amusing and interesting your ride when jumping

Shorten the ride's stirrups one or two holes. Check girths.
1. Judging when the horse will take off. Approach the jump in canter, saying, "One – One – One," as the leading foreleg comes to the ground then three strides away say, "Three, Two, One," and as the horse takes off, "Go." Even more fun is to sit quietly until three strides out then say, "Hip, Hip, Hip, Huy-Ray!" "Hur," as the horse takes off and a good loud "Ray," in the air! More advanced riders can see how far from the jump they can judge take off correctly; for instance, "5, 4, 3, 2, 1, Go." A marker placed approximately at four strides out will help the less experienced to know where to start counting. The jump can be really tiny or a decent size and upright or spread for the more experienced.
2. Left right centre. Three different types of jump of a small size (from poles on the ground for beginners) to a decent size for the experienced. One fence straight ahead, the other two one each side of it and set at an angle to it, uprights with no wings. Place two markers, six to eight strides from the fence straight ahead (nearer to it for more experienced riders). They approach in turns as their name is called, at walk, trot or canter according to their ability (but start at walk so that they get the feel of it) and as they pass through the two markers you say, "Left, right or centre." They have to do several half-halts if they are to turn left or right and succeed in getting over the centre of the named fence. If you have a ride of varying ability have one easier fence. This exercise teaches both control in turning and how to ride on at a fence. It is useful practice for show jumping or cross-country.

3. Jumping from walk. Not for beginners or very lazy horses or horses which refuse. They must want to jump. Walk into a fence of a size to suit the riders – it can be a good size jump. Walk straight at the fence, the riders sitting slightly forwards so that they will stay "with" the horse when it breaks into trot. Do not interfere with or influence the horse in any way. Swing forward from the hips as the horse takes off. Some horses will only trot in the last two strides and then put in a big round jump, others may put in one or two strides of canter. The horse has to think and sort itself out and the rider has to follow the horse. (Horses which rush should not approach the jump straight. They should come in from the side in a short tight turn so that they have only two strides at most before the jump.) The rider must be very agile to get forward quickly with the horse.
4. Pair jumping. For safety all jumps must be clearly divided into two halves by something such as a large cone, or two clearly separate jumps must be built side by side to prevent horses crossing and causing accidents. One of the pair must be "Boss" and give the orders for when they are going to trot and go on. The other must obey their orders and stay level knee to knee. Pair them off so that ponies of the same temperament and stride are together. Next, send the pair to opposite sides of the school. They are now approaching from different directions but must both be in the air over the jump at the same time so the riders need to have accurate control and good judgement of pace. For safety's sake make sure that everyone keeps to the left and knows which their left is – or put red ribbons on one fence and blue on the other and tell them which colour is theirs. This can be run as a competition, the ride judging and marks being lost for every length the horses are apart. The two ways of jumping can be combined for the result.
5. Wheel.
    a. Four long poles are used to form the spokes of the wheel resting on a round can or "block" as the central hub. Use four "blocks" or cans for the outer ends. This can be used with poles on the ground for beginners. Challenge: which is the quickest way to jump round all four poles? No two consecutive poles must be jumped in the same direction without a circle or turn in between. There are endless possibilities.

b. Jumping the "Vs". The same formation can be used to jump over the centre of the four "Vs" formed by the poles. With very careful organisation the ride can be divided into two or four and can each approach and jump the centre "V" in turns from two or four different directions. Having landed they must be told to circle out round their opposite group before halting in their place. Each group will end up where the opposite group were standing waiting.

6. Team game. Build three wide jumps each divided by a marker or six jumps side by side in pairs. All must be built so that they can be jumped from both directions. The teams stand at opposite short ends of the school facing inwards. A marker is placed near each team in front of them but with sufficient room for a horse to circle round it. The jumps are parallel with the short sides of the school, one central on the BE line, one a little nearer one short side, one a little nearer the other. Everyone must keep to their left as they approach the jump from whichever end. At the word, "Go," the first team member from each side has to jump the left side of one jump, then go round the cone in front of their team, before jumping the left side of another jump, then round the cone to jump the left side of the third jump. They must then touch the next team member who then does the same thing. The fences can be jumped in any order but always on the left side. Only two people are ever jumping at once and they must be warned to look and think and not get in each other's way. This game can be done with beginners with poles on the ground. Because of the sharp turns and amount of accurate control needed in this game left, right, centre is best used first as a preparation. Half-halts and smooth accurate turns must be explained and encouraged. Being rough and hauling ponies about is penalised by heavy penalty marks or elimination!

7. The pen. An oblong of jumps should be set at one non-jumping stride and two non-jumping strides respectively. Check on distances and use those suitable to the size of most of the animals in your ride. This formation can be jumped as straight through doubles or in at the short end and out left or right at the top of the long end or in at the long end and out at the short end. The pen is very versatile and can be used at different heights to suit everyone from beginners to the more

advanced. It can be shortened up so that the "long" way becomes one non-jumping stride and the short way a bounce – jump-jump. More experienced riders and "onward-bound" horses will need the longest distances, inexperienced riders or very quiet animals the shorter ones.

8. Figure-of-eight jumping. One jump with lots of space round it. The figure-of-eight can be jumped in two ways.

a. So that the round circles of the figure-of-eight are each side of the jump itself or so that the round circles of the figure-of-eight are round the uprights of the jump. Big circles can give a straight approach. Small circles will give an approach at an angle as acute as the rider wants to make it. This is suitable for beginners with a pole on the ground or more advanced riders with a proper jump. The emphasis here is on learning change of balance before change of direction and of course half-halts come in in a big way. More advanced riders doing this exercise at canter will learn most from it. If they change their weight, towards the new direction which the horse will take on landing, just before take off and use the aids for canter on that new lead the horse should change legs in the air over the jump and land smoothly in canter on the correct lead for the new direction. It needs precision riding, accurate timing and great "feel" on the rider's part. It is excellent practice for show jumping against the clock and for cross-country riding where sharp turns and changes of direction are required through combination fences.

b. Work through jumping stands alone to practise approaches, warning and preparing the horses and riding a good track. Make a figure-of-eight round two sets of stands. In approach they must never go over the centre line of the fence or they will have to make a "wiggle" to correct the approach and so unbalance the horse. Progress to a single pole on the ground, then cross-poles (which encourage horses to go straight to the centre). If the riders sit upright over jumps say, "There is a very low arch over the jump made of stone. If you don't tuck your head down you will be knocked unconscious – mind your head, get it down." This is not very correct as they tend to round their backs instead of having a flat back but it does help to get them forward.

9. Three jumps in a row, 6–8m (19.5–26.25ft) apart. Practise for accuracy and control. Stay on the same rein. Jump the last jump first coming in on a curve, go away on the same curve taking a track which will lead the horse to the middle of the centre jump, keeping the same curve and direction take a track which will lead the horse to the centre of the first jump and then finish on the same curve in the same direction. Do the same in the opposite direction on the other rein. With experienced horses and riders changes of direction (and therefore changes of leg if they are in canter) can be brought into the patterns. This way of jumping helps horses which rush their fences as it can be done at walk and then trot, using the turns to slow the horse down.
10. Coloured ribbons can be hung on a thin twig stuck into any jump and the rider must collect the ribbon as they go over the jump. Make sure that it is at a suitable height to be within reach. If the ribbon is big some animals may be frightened when the rider picks it up.
11. By now your ride should have developed an "eye" for when a rider is sitting correctly when jumping and is going with their mount. Have a jumping competition judged on style of rider only. Either give points for each jump or to make the arithmetic easier an overall mark for general impression and performance – one total mark for each rider. The ride must judge with you and decide the mark to be given. Even ten to twelve year olds enjoy taking a real interest in this and discussing the good and bad points of a round. The rider on the best jumper will not necessarily win. A rider who has a refusal through no obvious fault on their part and who copes well and really rides and gets over in style on the second attempt should not lose marks. The track ridden should flow and the approach be accurate.
12. Competitions for the horse/pony who jumps the most stylish flowing, clear round, using its head, neck and back, rounding, meeting fences in its stride and keeping an even rhythm. Adults and children learn from and enjoy these competitions.

Pony Club camp dismounted

Give each pupil a stable management subject to talk about for three minutes. If at camp, they can be given the subject the day before and be encouraged to collect relevant objects to show the other pupils. This arrangement makes it much more interesting for them.

Showing

Pony Club rallies, riding club rallies or camps where you will perhaps spend several days instructing the same riders are an ideal time to include "showing" in your teaching.

Many people, children and adults, go to local shows never having had a lesson on the subject. They have no idea how to ride a horse to give an individual show nor how to show a horse in-hand.

A suggestion for their individual show which can be used if the judge has not given specific requirements is:
1. Walk out to a clear space in front of the judge.
2. Trot a figure-of-eight of two 20m circles.
3. Start to canter a figure-of-eight where the two circles meet and going on the same rein as the last trot circle. This will then have been the preparation for canter and give a chance to get the correct bend and balance ready for it. Use half-halts coming towards the point where the two circles meet ready for trot sitting. Straighten the horse, half-halts, change the bend, half-halts and canter the second circle on the other rein. Use as few steps of sitting trot as possible to produce a smooth, unhurried change of canter lead.
4. Sitting trot after the figure-of-eight, walk and halt in front of the judge.
5. Drop the reins on the horse's neck to show that it is both calm and well mannered.
6. Smile at the judge and give a small bow.

In ridden classes, saddles may have to be taken off and riders asked to show their horse in-hand – walk and trot it out for the judge. Reins should be held in the right hand. The end of the reins and the cane (correct for showing) should be in the left hand.

The judge wants to look first at the animal's conformation. It should be lead out in front and halted with the horse sideways on and about 3m (10ft) away from the judge. Halt so that the animal's longer side is towards the judge. (The foreleg nearer the judge should be a little in advance of the other foreleg and the hind leg nearer the judge should be a little behind the other hind leg.)

If the halt hasput the horse wrong for this position, the leader should push the animal back a step with one hand on the rein or nose and one on the point of the shoulder of the leg the animal should step back with.

The leader should now stand in front of the animal's head, but avoid obstructing the judge's view. A few pony nuts or some grass held under the animal's nose then carried back a little towards its chest will make it arch its neck and look interested, giving a better picture.

The judge may feel the animal's fore and hind legs, then hold its tail to one side to look at its hocks before progressing to the other side. The leader should now push the horse back a step so that, once more, its long side is towards the judge.

This way of presenting a horse to the judge also applies when the class is for in-hand (unridden) classes.

The judge will now probably ask for the horse to be walked away and trotted back. The leader should then walk away 30–40m (33–44yd) and turn the animal away from the judge (so that the leader walks round the horse – not the horse round the leader).

On the return, trot straight at the judge, the leader running up level with the horse's shoulder. Keep trotting at the judge who will move to one side as the horse trots on, watch as it passes, then step behind so that he or she can see its action at trot from the rear. For this reason the leader must keep the horse trotting straight for some distance after passing the judge and before walking and returning to their place in line.

This way of trotting out for the judge is also used in the in-hand classes.

Riders will then remount and be told to walk in a circle round the judge. They will be called in, one at a time, in order of merit to line up for the presentation of prizes.

Conclusion

I hope that this book has helped you with the basics of teaching, given you some new ideas and encouraged you to look, listen and think and so continue to improve the quality of your instructing and understanding of horse and rider.

Index

Note: page numbers in *italics* refer to illustrations

above-the-bit *110*, 112–3
accident book 16, 17–18
adult riders 163–4
ankles, weak 42–3
approach, jumping 148, 155–7
arms of rider 30–2
assessment of new riders 10–11
    for hacking 13, 136–7

back, rider's
    collapsed 33–7
    hollow 37–9, 83
    length 29
back problems, horse 69–70, 99, 101–2
barrels/cones for teaching 128–30
beginners 44
    adult 163–4
    canter 11, 94–6
    jumping 147–52
    rising trot 84–8
    sitting trot 11, 78–81
behind the movement 86–8
bend for circles/turns 91–2
bending 73, 128
bitless bridles 47
bits 44–5
    bradoon 124
    cheek snaffle 45–6, 107–8,

curb 124–5
French snaffle *46*, 47, 108
Fulmer snaffle 108
jointed ring snaffle 45–6, 107
safety 8, 10
straight bar snaffle 108
bolting 105
boys, teaching 165–6
bradoon bit 124
breastgirth 27
breastplate 26–7, 146
bridge, reins
    for control 103–4
    reins in one hand 35, 172–3

canter
    aids 97–8
    beginners 11, 94–6
    class lessons 95–6
    correct lead 97, 98, 99–101
    disunited 99
    hacking 13–14, 137–8
    jumping 157–60
    on lunge 82–3
    maintaining 98
    on the bit 112
    safety in 9–10, 11–12
    serpentines 92

185

Index

step sequence 94
transition 66, 69–70, 172
uphill 94–5
cavalletti 9
cavesson noseband 121–2
child rider
  boys 165–6
  half halts 90
  position 168–70
  reins 8, 50–1, 171
  trotting 169–71
  teaching safety 135, 168
  whips 59
  see also Pony Club rallies, class games/exercises
circles
  correct bend 91–2
  downward transitions 113
  hand position 64–5, 92
  serpentine 93
  use of whip 60
  using barrels/cones 128–9
class games/exercises, on flat
  chain 172
  cogs in wheel 175
  handy pony 176
  Mr McGregor's garden 176
  pairs 175
  plait 175
  potato picking 173
  reins in one hand 172–3
  ribbons 176
  scavenger hunt 174–5
  scissors 175
  serpentines 92–3
  Western riding 173–4
class games/exercises, jumping
  competitions 181

figure 8 180
jumping from walk 178
jumps in a row 180
left-right-centre 177
pair jumping 178
the pen 179–80
ribbons 180
take off 177
team games 179
wheel 178
class lessons
  barrels/cones 128–30
  canter 95–6
  finishing 5
  planning 1, 18
  sitting trot 79–80
  size 1–2
  trotting poles 139–43
conformation of horse 21, 26–7
conformation of rider
  ankles 42–3
  arms 30–2
  collapsed back 33–7
  crooked seat 28, 39–40
  hollow back 37–9, 83
  legs 29–30, 41–2
  long back 29
  overweight 32
  round shoulders 32–3
  short back 29
  toes 30, 40–1
contact , 49–50, 109
  double bridle 125
  jumping 146–7, *148*, 159
control
  bulging shoulder 59, 105–7
  jumping 152
  loss of 104–5

Index 187

outside rein 106–7
  steadying/stopping 103–4
  stride 104–5
corrections,
  trying out 2–4, 19
  wording 2–4, 40, 167, 169
crupper 25
curb bit 124–5
curb chain 125, *126*

danger, potential 7–10, 15–16, 18
  on foot 17
  hacking 13–15
  jumping 12, 18
  new pupils 10–12
  tack 7–8, 10
  teaching about 135, 168
diagonals 88–90
dismounted lessons 16–17, 88, 181–2
distances
  doubles 156
  trotting poles 139–40, 141, *143*
double bridle
  advantages of 126–7
  bradoon 124
  contact 125
  curb bit 124–5
  curb chain 125, *126*
  lip strap 125
  reins 123–4, 125–6
doubles, jumping 154–8

escorts, hacking 14–15, 137
exercises 2–4, 19
explanations 2–4, 5–6

falls
  accident book 16, 17–18
  avoiding 15–16, 18
  causes 12–13
  dealing with 15, 16
  hacking 13–15
flash noseband 122–3

girth checking 7–8, 10
gripping, rider's legs 74–6

hacking 136–8
  assessing rider for 13, 136–7
  canter 13–14, 137–8
  escorts 14, 15, 137
  falls 13–15
  see also traffic, riding in
half–halts 66–7, 90
halt 67
hands
  in canter 96
  circles and turns 64–5, 92
  crossing over neck 71–2
  position 3–4, 30–2, 62–5
  softening *63*, 64
  in transitions 65–70
  see also whips
head, rider 34 36–7
hollow back 37–9, 83
horse
  behaviour 9–10
  conformation 21, 26–7
  school *see* school horse

instructor 1, 2–4, 95, 167

jumping
  adults 163–4
  approach 148, 155–7
  beginners 147–52

188 Index

canter 157–60
contact 146–7, *148*, 159
control 152
courses 152–4
doubles 154–8
forward seat 147–9
holding mane 144–6, 149–50
landing *150*
neckstrap 146
position *144–5*
preparation of rider 147–9
refusals 147, 151, 154, 156–7, 160–1
rushing fences 161–2
school horses 151
young horses 162–3
jumps 154–8
safety 9, 18

kicking, control of 135–6
knees, rider's 74–5

leg aids 72–3
circles and turns 91–2
spurs 73–4
whip use 61–2
leg yielding 130
legs, rider's
correct position 72–3
gripping 74–6
rider conformation 29–30, 41–2
lip strap 125
lunge horse 80, 81–3
lungeing the rider 81–4

"magic wand" whip 59
mane, holding 144–6, 149–50
Market Harborough 119–120, *121*
martingales

Market Harborough 119–120, *121*
running 119, *120*
standing 119, *121*
mounting 54

neck, rider 34, 36–7
neck reining 173–4
neckstrap, jumping 146
nosebands
cavesson 121–2
drop 122
flash 122–3

on the bit 108–13
overbent *110*
overweight rider 32

pelvis *see* seat bones
personality of teacher 1
point straps 25
Pony Club rallies 5–6, 109, 135
boys' ride 165–6
dismounted 181–2
jumping 152–3, 177–81
showing 182–3
teaching safety 135, 168
youngest ride 166–71
see also class exercises/games
position of rider 19–27
jumping *144–5*
rising trot *85*, 86–8
saddles 22–5, 84, 86–7, 169
sitting trot 78–9
see also conformation, rider; seat
praise 4–5, 167
pulling horse, control 103–4
pupils
names 4, 5

Index

new 10–12, 13, 136–7
own horses 9, 44, 135, 152–4, 162–3
taught as individuals 4–5

"question mark" shape of rider 34–5

rallies *see* Pony Club rallies
refusals, jumping 147, 151, 154, 156–7, 160–1
rein back 116–18
reins
  bridge *35*, 103–4
  bulging shoulder control 106–7
  child rider 8, 50–1
  length 21, 31–2, 47–50
  double bridle 123–4, 125–6
  grass 51–3
  one hand *35*, 172–3
  overuse 171
  rubber 47
  Western riding 173–4
  see also contact
rising trot
  beginners 81, 84–7
  common faults 87–8
  diagonals 88–90
  dismounted lesson 88
  position *85*, 86–8
  serpentines 92
round shoulders 32–4, 83
rushing fences 161–2

saddles
  correction to fitting 23, 86–7
  fitting 25–7
  position 22–5, 84, 86–7, 169
  safety 7–8, 10
  seat shape *24*

trees 8, 25
safety
  checking tack 7–8, 10
  hacking 13–15, 136–8
  kicking 135–6
  on foot 17
  jumping 12, 18
  new pupils 10–12
  teaching about 135, 168
  whips 58–9
school horse
  jumping 11, 151
  on lunge 80, 81–3
  voice 95
seat
  crooked *28*, 39–40
  fork 48, 77, 83
  forward 147–9
seat bones 19–22, 91–2
serpentine circles 93
serpentines 90–3, 128
short back, rider 29
shortening stride 104–5, 141, 143
shoulder, bulging 59, 105–7
shoulders, round 32–4, 83
showing 182–3
shying
  control 132–5
  traffic 130–1, 134–5
  whip 60–1
sitting in balance 23, *60*, 79, 86, 168–70
sitting trot 78–81
  child rider 169–71
  on lunge 83–4
spurs 73–4
stirrups
  crossing 81
  riding without 11, 83–4

safety 8, 10
weak ankles 42–3
stirrup length 76–8, 84
  hollow back 38–9
  jumping *145*, 147
  unequal 41–2
stride, lengthening/shortening 104–5, 141, 143

tack, inspecting 7–8, 10
teacher *see* instructor
toes of rider 40–1, 29–30
traffic, riding in 130–2, 134–5
transitions 65–70
  canter 69–70, 97–8
  downward 66–9, 112–13
  halt 67
  upward 66
trot
  on-the-bit 111
  step sequence 84–5
  see also rising trot; sitting trot
trotting poles 9
  class ride 139
  distances 139–40, *141*, 143
  fan shape 139, 142–3
  stride 141, 143
  in walk 143

turn on the forehand 113–15
turn on the haunches 115–16

vision of horse in traffic 130, *131*
voice of instructor 2–4, 95, 167

walk
  jumping from 178
  on the bit 110–11
Western riding 173–4
whip
  changing 57–8
  child rider 59
  circles 60
  leg aids 61–2, 72
  long 59–62
  "magic wand" 59
  mounting 54
  position 54–7, 60
  safety 58–9
  short 59

young horse
  ABC of Breaking and Schooling Horses 162
  canter 70
  jumping 162–3
  in traffic 131–2